**ALSO BY C**

(Just As Well) It's Not About The Bike

Escape To California

# FERTILISATION TO FATHERHOOD

## THE PREGNANCY DIARY OF A FIRST-TIME DAD

# CHRIS ATKIN

Fertilisation To Fatherhood
The Pregnancy Diary Of A First-Time Dad

Copyright © 2023 Chris Atkin
All rights reserved

Chris Atkin asserts the moral right to be identified as the author of this work.

Cover design by Donika Mishineva
www.artofdonika.com

First edition. ISBN: 978-1-8384485-5-4

www.chrisatkinonline.com

*To our baby, who one day will no doubt think this book contains far too much information.*

"...the only point of keeping a journal was to concentrate on the personal, the diurnal minutiae and forget the great and significant events in the world at large. The newspapers cover all that anyway - we don't want to know that Hitler invaded Poland, we're more curious about what you had for breakfast - unless you happened to be there of course when Hitler invaded Poland and your breakfast was interrupted."

– Any Human Heart by William Boyd

# PREFACE

Many people might question what the diary of a first-time father-to-be has to offer. As will become abundantly clear, this book does not try to compete with the in-depth manuals already available to the expectant dad. If one of your friends has recently become a father, don't be surprised if a few of these tomes are handed to you unread. Even if you have the best of intentions, you will likely do the same after reading as little of the guides as they did.

What I hope this book does do is provide some useful information, a little humour and a large dollop of reassurance. Just remember that everyone's pregnancy journey is unique and your partner and baby's development may differ to how it unfolded for us.

Men may spend much of the nine months on the sidelines, but that doesn't mean their role should be overlooked. Like a boxing trainer in a fighter's corner, what he says and what he does makes a difference.

*Week 1*

## Day 0 - Saturday, 27 August

I can't say too much, but it was great fun. And unexpectedly life-changing.

*Week 2*

## Day 7 - Saturday, 3 September

My wife Sarah and I attended the wedding of the friend who first introduced us. In my inebriated state I completely forgot Sarah might be pregnant. I teased her that she was dodging drinks and shamed her into downing a shot of tequila.

In hindsight, this was a mistake.

*Week 3*

## Day 14 - Saturday, 10 September

After leisurely finishing a cup of coffee over breakfast, Sarah wondered aloud if it was worth giving one of those pregnancy tests she bought a while ago a try. She returned a few minutes later and handed me the instructions to the test in Czech in her haste to verify the result. When we finally found the English translation, the result was unambiguous.

We had been trying to get pregnant for little more than a month so it wasn't a total shock. However, both of us have friends who had taken several months to conceive and we'd braced ourselves for a long journey before we even reached the pregnancy start line. So I am pleased, surprised and, I'm ashamed to admit, a little bit proud with the speed of the conception.

Sarah and I had always wanted to have children. Yet neither of us were particularly enthralled by the prospect of having babies.

I looked forward to going snorkelling with our son or daughter on holiday, teaching them how to make an igloo and watching classic films with them. But you can't do any of these things with a baby. You just get a lot less sleep.

Some couples become broody over time or become aware of a gaping hole in their lives where they feel a child should be. That was never the case for us. We could have continued our comparatively carefree existence, going on adventures near and far and making the most of spontaneous plans. We weren't spring chickens any more though. Doctors describe pregnancies involving women over the age of 35 as 'geriatric'. Sarah would soon be turning 34 and I was only a few months behind her. If I didn't want to be carting children off to university into my sixties, we needed to get a move on.

When Sarah showed me the positive test, I thought of how lucky we were, but instinctively, also of a clock counting down the less than nine months we had together until our lives changed forever. I was struck too by the similarity between the results of our pregnancy test and a Covid test. The 'two lines means you're positive' no longer carries such great connotations as it did pre-pandemic. Indeed, having caught the virus earlier that summer, less than a fortnight before our wedding party, I was less nervous about the result of this test, which didn't have a celebration three years in the planning hanging in the balance.

"Perhaps it's a false negative," Sarah said. "These were cheap tests - I don't know if we can trust them."

I couldn't help but think this was one of those occasions when it might have been worth spending the money to know one way or the other. But I held my tongue. "Why not take another and see if it agrees?"

The only problem was that unlike a Covid test, where your nose and mouth are only a plastic swab away, the bladder needs time to refill. And drinking lots of water only dilutes the hormone the pregnancy test is supposed to detect. So, like a drug tester waiting for a dehydrated athlete at the end of a race, we waited, full of anticipation, for a B sample.

We filled the time by calculating the birth date, which we estimate will be 27 May. Research has shown that children born in autumn are more likely to achieve sporting success, so we've missed a trick here, but I'm aware our genes have already tipped the scales heavily against the chance of them achieving sporting immortality. Or at least mine have. Sarah was briefly a GB athlete, but as the sport in question was wallball, I'm not sure it holds much currency.

"When do people normally share the news? Is it after 12 weeks?" I asked.

"I've no idea. I just know I can't go to all the weddings over the next few weeks without people noticing that I'm not drinking."

"Yeah, that might be tricky."

We lapsed into silence, realising we might need to come clean earlier than we'd have chosen to.

"Let's not worry about it," Sarah instructed, rising to her feet. "We'll wait and see what the second test says."

Sarah returned five minutes later with a test that emphatically showed she was pregnant. The second line denoting a positive test was much thicker and more defined this time around. She was becoming more pregnant by the minute.

*Week 4*

## Day 16 - Monday, 12 September

Sarah called the doctor and self-consciously informed them she was pregnant to find out the next steps. The first, she was told, was to study the list of foods she should cease eating.

While it won't be difficult to avoid marlin, quail eggs and pheasant, the limit on cups of coffee and the ban on soft cheese was a bitter pill to swallow. We still have blocks of frozen brie sitting in the freezer from our wedding 10 weeks ago.

## Day 17 - Tuesday, 13 September

A wedding invitation from my close friend, Peter, arrived with details of a glamorous ceremony to be held in Croatia next spring. My heart sank when I saw the date was set for 27 May.

Even allowing for the fact that most first-borns arrive late, I know I won't be able to attend.

## Day 18 - Wednesday, 14 September

After a bit of online research, Sarah casually tells me over breakfast that she's not actually two and a half weeks pregnant, but five weeks. I choked on my cereal. Not because I'm worried some other bloke has got there first, or because it's ruined the numbering of days in this diary, but because the imaginary countdown clock in my mind just started accelerating.

It turns out the nine-month gestation time frame weirdly doesn't begin from the moment of conception. Instead it's from the date of the woman's last period. We quickly recalculate that the due date will be around 13 May. On the plus side, this means the baby is marginally more likely to be good at sport, but it doesn't much help my chances of being able to fly to Croatia for 27 May.

*Week 5*

### Day 38 - Thursday, 15 September

Sarah's spending more and more time down internet rabbit holes. I can't blame her - I'd do the same if I learned I had someone growing inside me. Today she informed me our baby is now the size of an orange seed. Up until this point, I'd pictured it as a tiny clump of cells, so I was shocked to learn it's already so big.

### Day 39 - Friday, 16 September

For the first time during the pregnancy, Sarah experienced mild stomach cramps. I suggested she relaxed by watching *Frozen Planet II* while lying on the sofa. I'm not sure watching a grizzly bear maul week-old ox calves in the Arctic Tundra helped to set her mind at ease though.

## Day 40 - Saturday, 17 September

"Wowww! The train is moving so fast!" Sarah exclaimed, sitting bolt upright in the middle of the night.

I tactfully agreed and she lay back down and carried on sleeping. In the nearly six years we've been together, Sarah has never previously exhibited any unusual nocturnal behaviour. I hope it isn't a quirk of pregnancy.

## Day 41 - Sunday, 18 September

When I mentioned her antics overnight, Sarah said that as my sleep will soon be interrupted a lot, "I may as well get used to it."

I had considered going teetotal in a show of solidarity with my pregnant wife, but my good intentions lasted all of a week. Tonight I cracked open the solitary beer that's been winking at me every time I've opened the fridge. At the end of the day, there's no need for us both to go without.

*Week 6*

## Day 42 - Monday, 19 September

Queen Elizabeth II's funeral was held today. The occasion leads me to reflect that while our baby may have missed out on including Her Majesty when they count how many monarchs they've lived through, they will at least be able to claim they were conceived in the second Elizabethan age. Which is not something all of their peers will be able to say. Not that they will care much in 2110 when they are living in a republic under the sea.

## Day 43 - Tuesday, 20 September

Sarah's joy at so far being unaffected by morning sickness has dimmed slightly. She's read some studies indicating that women with nausea and vomiting during the first trimester have a lower risk of miscarriage than women without these symptoms.

According to the National Health Service, among people who know they are pregnant 1 in 8 pregnancies end in miscarriage. A few of our friends have experienced this unimaginable sadness and knowing it could happen to us continues to temper our excitement. Despite impacting the lives of so many people, miscarriage remains a taboo subject. It's an intensely private matter, but raising awareness and eradicating the myths around it is vital.

On a lighter note, an old wives' tale suggests pregnant women who experience morning sickness are more likely to give birth to a girl. While Sarah believes she's carrying a boy, I've a strong hunch they're a girl. It goes without saying we just want the baby to be healthy, but Sarah would be overjoyed to have twins so that we could raise two children without the need for a second pregnancy. I'm less keen on the possibility. Keeping one newborn baby happy and alive will be tough enough.

## Day 44 - Wednesday, 21 September

"Happy birthday!" I said over the phone to my dad.

"Thanks Old Lad. 61 years young and onto my second monarch. Anything new to report?"

"Oh, not much, you know." I tell myself this isn't a lie - just a sidestep. But I still feel deeply duplicitous. I intend to tell my parents in person when we're a bit further down the line, but doing so will require me to avoid accidentally spilling the beans in the meantime.

## Day 45 - Thursday, 22 September

Morning sickness has kicked in. Or maybe it hasn't. Sarah might just be under the weather. Either way, I don't dare suggest her symptoms are psychosomatic.

"You know what's rubbish about morning sickness?" she asked.

"The nausea?"

"Well, yeah, that. But it's the fact it doesn't go away at noon. I bet a man came up with the name. A woman wouldn't have."

I didn't know my wife had an angry feminist side. She must be pregnant.

## Day 46 - Friday, 23 September

Sarah's started to notice a shortness of breath. This seemed inevitable in the weeks prior to the birth when she would be the size of our hatchback, but neither of us had anticipated she would be feeling like this so soon. Especially when she'd spent the day sitting at the kitchen table.

The phenomenon occurs because a woman's diaphragm rises by as much as 4cm during the first trimester (the first 14 weeks of pregnancy). This limits how deeply she can breathe - at the precise point when she needs to be increasing her oxygen intake.

## Day 47 - Saturday, 24 September

We've been rumbled.

When we arrived at our friends' wedding, we'd optimistically clung to the hope that Sarah's temperance might slip under the radar. We should have known better. At 11.30pm, a friend who had been forced to leave our wedding for picking up a waitress - not in the sense of getting her number, but literally for giving her a fireman's lift - shared his suspicions with the group.

We considered coming clean, but, as we were already eight hours deep into the wedding reception, it wasn't the moment to announce that, yes, we were expecting and that no, we wouldn't be at Peter's wedding.

Fortunately, enough people saw Sarah charging her glass for the toasts during the wedding breakfast that our protestations were believed. Nevertheless, we know we'll face renewed questioning if we don't say something soon. A fortnight from now, we'll all meet up again for another friend's nuptials. Trying to reach the 12-week scan in secret appears to be impossible during the wedding season.

One girl in the pew behind us in the church had taken the opposite approach. She wasn't visibly pregnant and was only attending the service with her partner. But in case anyone was wondering, she'd pinned a 'Baby on board' badge to her lapel. If she did so in the hope of sparking a conversation, she wasn't going to get it from us.


### Day 48 - Sunday, 25 September

Upon returning from the wedding in Manchester, we moved back into our house in Cambridge. We'd let it out two years ago when Sarah was offered a Fellowship at Stanford University in California and we hadn't been back since. Now the tenants had departed, we began unpacking all of the belongings we'd hidden in the loft.

Boxes of kitchenware and old suitcases filled with books soon occupied every inch of the floor. When Sarah needs to reach the bathroom, she must now complete an obstacle course to get there.

For a long time I'd looked forward to being reunited with our home office. The room isn't big enough to fit a double bed, but, unlike the tiny studio apartment we rented in the US, it has an internal door. Knowing this refuge will soon need to be converted into a nursery made returning to it bittersweet. Particularly as the baby won't even appreciate the view from the window of the sparrows darting in and out of the vines that climb the wall.

*Week 7*

## Day 49 - Monday, 26 September

We spent the evening sitting in our bedroom unpacking under the light of a naked bulb. *Will we ever find the lamp shades?* As I reached into yet another cardboard Pandora's box, I picked up a framed photograph taken on the day of our lockdown wedding in August 2020. Due to the restrictions in place at the time, I couldn't get a visa to fly to America with Sarah without a marriage certificate, and after our nuptials had been delayed twice due to the nationwide ban on weddings, we both appear overjoyed to have finally tied the knot.

I glanced up from the photograph to watch Sarah. Her long brown hair hung loosely around her shoulders, casting half her face into darkness. The other half was lit up as if she was in a laboratory. In the unforgiving light, she looked tired and bored. She'd felt nauseous all day at work and was now going through the tedious task of sifting through folders of paperwork.

"What happened to this girl?" I asked, handing her the

photo. "You look so happy then."

"You impregnated me," Sarah replied, deadpan.

Nearly half a century of days into the pregnancy, the novelty is wearing thin.


## Day 50 - Tuesday, 27 September

It's my sister Katie's 32nd birthday. I rarely feel the passage of time when it's my birthday, but invariably do when Katie, who is 17 months younger than me, has hers. With every celebration, it becomes more difficult to deny the passing of my youth. After all, if Katie's 32, I'm running out of time to play for England.

This year Katie has made it particularly difficult for me to accept how fast things are changing by voluntarily choosing to spend her birthday in Ikea.

When I called her tonight, she demanded I serenade her with my best rendition of *Happy Birthday*. She laughed at how out of tune I was, before handing her phone over to Mum.

"We were about to cut into a chocolate cake," she told me.

"Well, I'm very jealous."

"So you should be. It's one of my best. Although, I'm fed up of making birthday cakes for thirty-somethings."

Sarah and I might not have been in a rush to have children, but Mum feels she's waited long enough.


## Day 51 - Wednesday, 28 September

Just when we were beginning to catch sight of the floorboards in our bedroom, I embarked on a 200-mile trip to collect a van's worth of my belongings my parents were itching to offload.

"Gosh," Sarah said as she walked through the front door and saw the fresh carnage I had unleashed in the living room. "How on Earth are we ever going to fit a pram in here?"

## Day 52 - Thursday, 29 September

Many of the boxes were still untouched when we received a call from the midwife the following morning. We'd expected the scheduled telephone appointment to be short and to the point, but we were guided through the various medical questions by a chatty woman who clearly relished her job as the wise owl dispensing advice to pregnant women in the local area.

The midwife saved the most delicate question to last, like a journalist obliged to ask a capricious celebrity about their role in a recent scandal.

"Now Sarah, this is very personal, and don't feel you have to answer this–"

I could feel Sarah bracing next to me on the sofa, readying herself for a question so difficult it caused even the unflappable midwife pause for thought.

"–but do you have any tattoos or piercings on your private parts?"

"No." Neither Sarah nor I could resist a smile.

"Ok, thanks," said the midwife, sounding equally relieved. "We only ask so that the midwife isn't shocked when you come in for your appointment. We've found it's helpful to know what to expect."

What have the midwives seen that has led to this line of questioning? Intimate tattoos depicting Brad Pitt's face? Genitalia emblazoned with swastikas? Or arrows alongside the words 'insert here'?

## Day 53 - Friday, 30 September

My parents have come to stay. When Sarah and I managed to move the conversation away from the plunging value of the pound and the exorbitant price of sofas, we broke the news about the pregnancy.

"Wow. Oh wow. Congratulations!" said Mum, thrilled but surprised.

Much like when I'd learned of the pregnancy, I could tell a hundred thoughts were flying through her mind. The one she reached for wasn't one we'd anticipated.

"How long had you been trying?"

"Carole!" reprimanded Dad.

"Not long," Sarah replied. "I didn't go back on the pill after our stuff was stolen in Mexico on our way back from America."

"That makes sense. Well - how exciting!"

When Mum was in the kitchen, Dad let slip she had secretly been buying baby clothes for "whenever they were needed". She admitted she'd also spent time considering possible grandmother names.

"I don't want something that makes me sound old. Nor anything too traditional. I was thinking something foreign might be fun."

"Ok..." I replied hesitantly.

"How about Abuelo?"

"As in grandfather in Spanish?"

"Fine, Abuela."

She could tell I wasn't convinced.

"What about Bibi?" she said, taking another sip of wine. "It's grandmother in Swahili."

"But you're not African?"

"No, but it's cute. If you're not keen, don't worry, I'll keep thinking."

Sarah and I had speculated what Mum's reaction to the pregnancy might be. Safe to say, neither of us had expected this.

### Day 54 - Saturday, 1 October

"I've decided what I want to be called," Mum announced as we ate breakfast.

"Ok," I said, trying to keep an open mind.

"I couldn't sleep last night after all the excitement, and it struck me that whatever name I choose, it will outlive us all. Long after your grandmother and I have gone, you'll still remember her as Nana. Likewise, your baby will remember me, not as Carole or Mum, but the name I'm going to be known as.

"That's true."

"I might change my mind again, but for now, I'm going for Lola."

"Lola?" I repeated, my eyebrows arching towards the ceiling.

"Yes, it's the term commonly used by Filipino children for their grandmothers," said Mum matter of factly.

"It's also the name we were going to call our cat."

"Well I've got there first - you can't call her that now!"

I look over to Dad, waiting for him to acknowledge that Mum's choice is a little odd. He though has no desire to be pulled into the discussion and is quietly singing the lyrics to *Lola* by the Kinks.

I speak over the chorus to ask him, "If she's going to be called Lola–"

"Who's she? The cat's mother?" Mum interjected.

"No, the cat's grandmother apparently," I responded dryly, before turning back to Dad, "then what are you going to call yourself?"

He ignored the question and continued singing, before finally breaking off. "You know the song is about meeting a transvestite in a nightclub?"

I confessed I did not.

"If Mum is Lola, I persisted, you can hardly be Grandpa. Grandpa and Lola sounds like you've got a fancy woman half your age."

He laughed, but Dad had decided to let Mum have her moment.

"You'd have to choose something that goes with Lola. What about Leo? Leo and Lola," I said, trying it out for size. "No, you sound like an indie folk band. What about Shola?"

"Shola?" The ridiculousness of the suggestion finally provoked a response.

"As in former Newcastle striker Shola Ameobi," I explained, standing to load the plates into the dishwasher. "You'd be Shola and Lola."

"No," said Dad decisively.

So it looks like our children will call their grandfather a name that will either make him sound like a cradle snatcher or an indie frontman.


## Day 55 - Sunday, 2 October

Chocolate has suddenly lost its appeal to Sarah. This represents quite a turn of events because up until recently, she would have happily eaten chocolate for breakfast every day. Now the idea repels her. It's as if pregnancy has turned her into an adult.

Ginger is widely thought to reduce feelings of nausea, so before she left yesterday, Mum went out and bought Sarah every type of ginger-based food and drink she could find. This included ginger nut biscuits, ginger cordial, ginger ale, ginger lemon kombucha and plain old ginger root.

Unfortunately, it's all too sweet for Sarah's palate at present.

Instead, she craves the salty, savoury crunch of salt and vinegar crisps. As I dislike the flavour, Sarah can't point the finger when supplies run low. But neither can I cast aspersions when the Dairy Milk now goes awol.

*Week 8*

**Day 56 - Monday, 3 October**

Sarah made her first in-person visit to the doctors to see a midwife, where she was asked a series of questions by an absent-minded trainee.

"Are you paraplegic?"

"No," replied Sarah, thinking the girl could have guessed as much when Sarah walked into the room.

"Do you have pre-eclampsia? (This is a serious pregnancy-related condition causing high blood pressure.)"

"Err...I don't know. Do you not tell me that?"

"Oh yes, you're right," the trainee admitted, looking down at her sheet. "Let's measure your BMI and blood pressure."

As she stood to leave, Sarah was handed a booklet called *Mothers and Others*. The culturally sensitive publication is predominantly about postnatal care and contained more breasts than a lads' mag. Breastfeeding felt like a long way off, but it highlighted how much we had to learn.

**Day 57 - Tuesday, 4 October**

"You're going to be an auntie."

"Shut up. What? No," said Katie. "How did this happen?

Actually don't tell me. This is amazing. Why did you let me go on about my gig so long when you had this to say?"

If our news wasn't enough to get her head spinning, I told her the name Mum wanted to go by. This was, of course, not just the name my children would call her, but Katie's future children too.

"Don't tell me it's French or something," she said.

"Oh, it's weirder than that."

"No."

"Lola."

"What? Are you serious? She can't be called that. For a start, babies can't pronounce L's so she'll at best be Ola. Gran Ola. Oh God."

"At least we know Dad should be called Yoghurt then."

She laughed ruefully. "If there's any doubt whether our parents are stranger than Sarah's, I think this settles it. Sarah's parents might live on a canal boat, but that's nothing compared to renaming yourself Lola."

After checking we weren't holding back any other revelations, Katie brought the call to a close so she could "take it all in".

I went into the kitchen, but 30 seconds later, popped my head back round the door. "Sarah, can you Whatsapp my parents to let them know the secret's out?"

There was no need. Dad had sent me a message saying Katie and Lola were already screaming with joy down the phone to one another.


### Day 58 - Wednesday, 5 October

A letter arrived informing us Sarah's 12-week scan will take place in early November. During the scan the sonographer will check the baby's heartbeat, identify the number of babies in the womb and give an estimated date of delivery, or to use a term less associated with Amazon packages, the baby's due date.

We're advised the scan may be "easier to perform if your bladder is not completely empty". Shows how much I know. I would have guessed the opposite to be true.

## Day 59 - Thursday, 6 October

At the end of a week in which I've told my family I'm going to be a father, my 32-year-old cousin announces they are changing their pronouns to she/them. It feels as if my family are a drugs bust away from a *Hollyoaks* episode.

Talking about changes, Sarah's breasts are - there is no delicate way to say this - markedly different to a few weeks ago. I'd eagerly anticipated their increase in size, but hadn't expected to notice changes to their weight and density so early in the pregnancy. For instance, the development of milk ducts makes it feel like she has memory foam in her chest. While I find these subtle variations diverting, Sarah's focus remains on battling through the ever-present nausea of 'morning' sickness.

## Day 60 - Friday, 7 October

We arrived in Devon the evening before another friend's wedding and told those attending about Sarah's pregnancy. Although it's still very early days it feels good to be open with everyone and pre-empt any further speculation.

## Day 61 - Saturday 8 October

When the wedding was first announced, we'd decided to camp in the grounds and assumed others would do likewise. No one did and we became minor celebrities at the wedding as the 'couple who camped'. Our attempts to persuade people that we weren't bonkers were inevitably undermined when they heard Sarah was pregnant. Still, we learned one surefire way to receive compliments on your appearance at a wedding is for fellow guests to learn you're staying in a tent.

During the wedding breakfast I went to the bar, where I found one of the groom's school friends standing alone. We'd met once, years before, and I remembered he lived in Cambridge.

"My wife's pregnant, so do you have anything we can put in her champagne glass?" he asked the barman.

The man nodded, taking the glass and opening the fridge to retrieve the Nosecco.

After the speeches a couple of hours later, I walked outside hoping to catch the last of the highly fortuitous, unseasonably sunny weather. However, I was too late. Night had arrived and the grounds were now illuminated by hundreds of fairy lights.

I walked past the guy I'd seen at the bar and, seeing he was alone, reintroduced myself.

"Hey, how are you?"

"Good thanks. Am I right in thinking you've been living in the States?"

"Yeah, we've just moved back."

"To Cambridge?"

"Yeah."

"Nice."

"Did I hear you say your wife's pregnant?"

"Yes..." he said, wrongfooted by the inadvertently sharp gear change. "We don't want to tell anyone until after the 12-week scan on Wednesday, so you're pretty much the only person here who knows."

Having lifted the shroud of secrecy regarding our own news, I'd walked straight into another.

## Day 62 - Sunday, 9 October

We were on the long drive back from Devon when Sarah said, "It's not fair. I should be feeling virtuous and full of energy. Yet even though I didn't drink last night, I feel like I'm hungover: nauseous and sleep-deprived.

For once, I *could* empathise.


*Week 9*


## Day 64 - Tuesday, 11 October

Since learning she was pregnant, Sarah has been using an app called Premom to follow the baby's growth.

"You know my uterus has doubled in size over the past nine weeks?" she asked me as we sat on the sofa.

"That sounds like a lot," I said, continuing to scroll through Twitter.

"...and my libido will apparently increase during the second trimester."

"Oh yes?" I said, looking up.

"That got your attention didn't it?"

"Yes," I admitted. "Did you make it up?"

"No." Sarah paused, realising she now needed to rein in my expectations of 14 weeks of carnal frenzy. "I imagine it really depends on whether the morning sickness has subsided by then. It's a bit of a mood killer."

She stood and went to make a cup of tea. While she was in the kitchen, I started looking through the app. Naturally, I went straight to the section on intercourse. The section is largely focussed on reassuring women that babies are both safe and unaware of what's going on during sex, but one part did draw my attention. It contained the following advice:

> "If you have oral sex, your partner should not blow into your vagina. Blowing air in the vagina can cause an embolism (blood vessels blocked by air bubbles), which can be fatal for the baby."

It had never even occurred to me to blow. Have I been doing it wrong all these years?

## Day 65 - Wednesday, 12 October

So far, the baby is doubling in size each week and is now the size of an olive with independently functioning lungs, kidneys, brain and liver. Sarah's womb has correspondingly grown to the size of a tennis ball, yet her waist appears to be unchanged. Which makes it all the harder to picture the developing life inside her.

## Day 66 - Thursday, 13 October

Sarah went for a blood test and submitted a urine sample as requested by the midwives. There's nothing unexpected about this, other than the fact they insisted she went to the hospital to have her blood taken. Perhaps they're frightened of finding a tattoo of Putin on her arm.

In the afternoon, Mum made a flying visit on her way back from Yorkshire. Cue a hurried attempt to hide all of the untouched ginger products she had bought Sarah. They may be opened one day, for Sarah's salt and vinegar crisp phase ended as quickly as it began. Such a passionate affair could never have lasted.

Sarah's decided roasted pumpkin seeds are what she

needs instead. After slaving away in the kitchen cooking an enormous batch of nutritious pumpkin and spinach risotto, I felt a little aggrieved that it was the seeds - roasted as an afterthought - that won the plaudits. And even the compliments I received for those were backhanded.

"Ooh, these are perfect for settling my stomach," she said, licking her fingers. "They're not very tasty–"

"Not very tasty?"

"No, they're very tasty. Just not too tasty," she said, backtracking with the grace of an undertaker arriving at the wrong church midway through a wedding.


## Day 67 - Friday, 14 October

Autumn has arrived. The sky is grey and while the leaves remain resolutely on the trees lining the River Cam, their days are numbered.

I was watching a novice rowing crew of university freshers struggle to turn their boat around when Sarah said, "It's funny, when we first found out I was pregnant the weeks seemed to whizz by–"

"That's because we found out you were three weeks more pregnant than we thought you were,"

"–and you have all of the excitement and everything," Sarah continued, "but now time until the 12-week scan seems to be dragging."

The weeks didn't feel like they were dragging to me. Since returning from California in June, we'd celebrated our wedding in July, conceived in August and moved house in September. All in between going on honeymoon, starting new jobs and attending four weddings.

"I know some friends went private and paid £80 for a scan before the 12-week mark, but I'm not sure it's worth it," Sarah said. "You have to wait until 12 weeks to check some things anyway and if everything is going well, then we've just spent £80 for peace of mind. If it isn't..." Sarah's voice trailed off. "But I'm still feeling sick every day, which suggests something's happening. Hopefully everything's alright."

"I'm sure it–"

"Like why is so much of my hair falling out?" she said, cutting across my well-meaning but baseless utterances of reassurance as she ran her hands through her hair. "I thought it was supposed to get thick and luscious during pregnancy?"

"So did I."

"I looked on the internet to find out if it was normal to lose more hair than usual during pregnancy," she said, tying her hair up. "But it's the same as with every symptom. There's just lots of conflicting advice, alongside warnings that it may indicate something is seriously wrong. You can see how people become hypochondriacs."

It was perhaps unfortunate timing to discover the blood test results had arrived when we returned home. The results were generally healthy, but the screening did produce an unexpected finding. Despite being rhesus-positive, Sarah has red cell antibodies. The attached note said only that "This result will delay the provision of blood". What this means is anyone's guess.

Our call to the midwives to ask for more information went to voicemail, so we started researching online. The problem with having red cell antibodies, we learned, is they might not recognise the baby as a welcome part of Sarah's body and, as a result, may attack it. The presence of these antibodies isn't necessarily anything to worry about, but neither of us can shake off the test result from the back of our minds.

In a moment of clarity, I realise the worries we have for

the health and wellbeing of our unborn child will not end at the 12-week scan, nor even at birth.

They will be with us for the rest of our lives.

## Day 69 - Sunday, 16 October

A lazy Sunday morning - *how many more do we have left?* - is interrupted at 8.30am by a much appreciated call from one of the midwives.

She agreed the detection of red cell antibodies is unusual given the fact Sarah is a first-time mother who hasn't previously had a blood transfusion, but told us not to worry as it wasn't considered "clinically significant".

In the afternoon we cycled across town to visit our friend Andy in his new house. For lunch, he served us delicious, large rare steaks, the likes of which we hadn't eaten for years.

## *Week 10*

## Day 70 - Monday, 17 October

Now we're back in the UK, Sarah's keen to resume playing the niche sport of fives. The sport is similar to wallball and involves hitting a hard ball with a gloved hand. Targeting the body of opponents is a legitimate tactic and Sarah's nose has never been quite the same since it was broken during a match a decade ago.

Any wonder I don't think it's a great time to make a return?

Sarah strongly believes being a woman shouldn't stop her from doing anything. And of course she's right. Up until this point, it hasn't prevented her from pursuing any of her passions. Before studying the male-dominated subject of engineering at university, Sarah travelled extensively and regularly beats me at a variety of sports.

She refused to accept that playing fives during pregnancy would put the baby's health at risk, and my efforts to convince her otherwise made me sound like a draconian duke desperate for an heir.

Seeking a second opinion, Sarah rang her parents. They agreed with me.

"Fine, but I'm still going to play tennis," she insisted.

"Is that wise?"

"Yes. Chris is just going to make sure he avoids my tummy."

"Hasn't he tried to avoid hitting the ball at you before though?" Sarah's dad asked, tongue in cheek. He was referring to a video in which I hit Sarah square in the chest while she filmed me practising my serve. The resultant clip achieved minor viral fame and we received £250 from the famously highbrow curator of online content, *SPORTbible*.

Loathe as I am to admit it, I will have to be more careful in the months ahead. I guess I'll stick to drop shots.


### Day 71 - Tuesday, 18 October

Sarah's gone off pumpkin seeds. Now she longs for crackers. I can't keep up.


### Day 72 - Wednesday, 19 October

Sarah suddenly remembered that, due to the harmful bacteria it may contain, undercooked meat is on the list of prohibited pregnancy foods. Amidst the excitement last Sunday of seeing Andy and the gargantuan steaks he'd cooked us, we completely forgot. The banned list is so long, it's worryingly easy to do. We vowed not to slip up again.

## Day 73 - Thursday, 20 October

I've had an argument with Sarah. We rarely argue, but when we do it invariably reflects poorly on me. This time is no different.

As the non-child bearing parent, I ought to assist Sarah where I can and I've no doubt that many men wait on hand and foot for their pregnant partners. I'm just not that nice.

A few weeks of concerted efforts to be the man I should be hasn't left me feeling warm and fuzzy. Just mildly irritated. Has Sarah forgotten where the dishwasher is? Is it too much to hope she might turn on Netflix while I'm fetching her a glass of water to drink in front of the TV?

I'm aware how petty this sounds. It's the kind of thing any reasonable person would let slide. At worst, they'd let off steam about it over a beer with a friend. But none of my closest friends have pregnant wives. And those that now have children are already nostalgic about the carefree existence of their child-free lives.

I can't escape the thought a precedent is being set and that the performing of these chores may soon stop being appreciated, or even noticed. Most likely I'll need to shoulder more, not less, of the burden during the remaining weeks of the pregnancy, and after the baby is born, doing so will be more important than ever. I fear I'll be the one drawing curtains and switching on lamps for the rest of our lives.

Sarah is hurt to learn the kind-hearted gestures of the past few weeks haven't been as unconditional as she had hoped.

After I locked up the house and turned off the lights, we went to bed in silence.

## Day 74 - Friday, 21 October

I woke from a vivid dream in which my teeth were falling out while I was playing football. Dreams about football aren't a rare occurrence, but imagining the loss of my teeth was a first for me. I looked up what it might mean and discovered that, according to psychiatrist Carl Jung, it hints at an upcoming transformation. This positive perspective on the impact of impending fatherhood is certainly preferable to other interpretations. These suggest that dreaming about losing one's teeth symbolises the lack of control we feel we have in our lives. Advocates for this analysis encourage individuals with such dreams to ask themselves if there is anything going on in their lives they feel powerless to influence. I don't need to.

## Day 75 - Saturday, 22 October

It doesn't quite top deciding to bring a child into the world, but Sarah and I make almost as great a commitment to each other by signing up for National Trust Life Family Membership. It costs a fortune, but we'll be laughing when we reach 53 years old and all future visits to stately homes are on the house.

"How many children do you have?" asked the administrator when I called to make the payment.

"How many can be included?"

"10."

"10! I don't think we're going to have that many." I looked across to Sarah, who was appalled by the idea.

"Can I have the names of those you would like to be included?" the administrator asked, trying a different tack.

"Err..." I paused, contemplating the names we might consider for our children. Between us we've ruled out so many, I doubted I could get to 10. I considered hedging my bets, but I came clean. "We haven't got any children yet," I said at last. The admission made me sound like a fastidious planner desperate for a discount.

"I'll put them down as Child 1 and Child 2 for now," she said patiently.

I've heard of worse names.

*Week 11*

## Day 77 - Monday, 24 October

Shortly before lunch, Sarah vomited for the first time since becoming pregnant. We'd been warned morning sickness is often worst approaching the end of the first trimester and it seems to be arriving right on cue.

Oh for the halcyon days when poor Sarah was just dry retching into the toilet bowl.

## Day 78 - Tuesday, 25 October

Sarah opted to work from home and in between sprints to the bathroom, attended a virtual meeting with her boss.

"You must forgive me if I'm not at my best," he told her, "I've just had my Covid booster jab."

"Don't worry, I've got mine later in the week," Sarah replied without thinking.

"Oh," he said, taken aback. "Ok."

Given the autumn booster is only available to the over-

50s, the medically vulnerable and carers, his surprise was understandable. Sarah doesn't want to tell him about the pregnancy just yet, but I doubt he'll be shocked when he learns of the news.

## Day 79 - Wednesday, 26 October

Now 11 weeks pregnant, Sarah's beginning to feel a little underwhelmed by her lack of a bump. While I suspect this may turn out to be much like the absence of morning sickness in that she will, in time, long for a flat stomach again, it's true that her height - Sarah's 5'10 - will mean she won't look obviously pregnant until much further down the line.

A friend of ours who's a doctor told Sarah it's common for first-time mothers to take a long time to show. This is because their abdominal muscles keep everything packed in. The second time around, these muscles have been stretched, causing a bump to appear much earlier in the pregnancy.

## Day 80 - Thursday, 27 October

Katie has come to stay. We were sitting in the living room, next to some freshly stacked bookshelves, when she told me, "You know our mother is currently washing all of the baby clothes and blankets we had when we were children?"

"What?"

"Yeah, they were all hanging from the bannisters when I left the house this morning."

"But why does she still have them?"

"No idea. Mum must have been keeping them all this time, ready for this moment," she said, putting down her mug of tea. "She's a bit disappointed though. They haven't come out as soft as she'd hoped."

"What did she expect? They're more than 30 years old! I've done you a favour having a baby first. Your future children won't know how lucky they are."

"Yeah, I definitely didn't want your old *Thunderbirds* duvet cover."

"It might be worth something now," Sarah said. "It'll be a collectors' item."

"I doubt it," I replied. "Those sheets have endured more than their share of sick and bed-wetting."

"Eurgh!"

"Let's not tell our child that."

"Are you coming to Battersea Park on Saturday?" Katie asked, keen to move on from the subject of my soiled sheets.

"No. What's happening?"

"Dad's doing a 10k run there. The friend he was doing it with has dropped out so I was going to go and support him." She paused. "You should take his friend's place!"

"I've still got a lot of unpacking to do…"

"Think how much he'd like it though."

"I haven't run that far for years."

"So? Come on, you know you should."

"You're going down to London anyway that afternoon, aren't you?" Sarah pointed out, wielding a sledgehammer to the wall of mental excuses I was hastily constructing.

"Well, yes…I'll have to think about it," I said, feeling a sense of filial obligation crystallising.


**Day 82 - Saturday, 29 October**

The first 8km of the run weren't too bad. But at that point any residual natural fitness I still possessed evaporated. As we reached the final 200 metres, I staggered and began to retch. Amidst the sensation of burning lactic acid and the fierce disappointment of watching Dad shuffle unassailably towards the finish line, I thought of Sarah, who is still dry retching daily. When I eventually stumbled over the finish line, I resolved to do more.

Housework that is. I'm sick to the back teeth of running.


*Week 12*


### Day 84 - Monday, 31 October

Our baby is apparently now able to form a fist and curl their toes. Which is about as much as I've been able to do without wincing since Saturday morning.


### Day 87 - Thursday, 3 November

The day of our 12-week scan finally arrived and we nervously entered a hospital waiting room full of heavily pregnant women.

"I feel like I shouldn't be here," Sarah whispered to me as she sat down.

"How do you think I feel?"

She laughed, but had no time to respond before a nurse ushered us in to see the sonographer.

After watching the moment be depicted many times on screen, it felt surreal to see the transparent gel squeezed onto Sarah's stomach in preparation for the scan. Her shallow breathing caused the mound of gel to rise and fall conspicuously, betraying her anxiety about what we might learn.

The sonographer pressed the transducer onto Sarah's skin and looked across at the monitor next to me. I followed her eyes. The baby's head, arms and legs flashed onto the black and white screen and everything was suddenly incontrovertibly real. There was, we quickly concluded to my relief, just the one baby.

I'd anticipated they would be relatively still, but they were moving around like a child on a twisty slide at a water park. One moment they were facing away from us, the next they were lying on their back, waving. From this position we could see their beating heart. In addition to fingers and toes, we also saw the baby's brain and their stomach, the latter of which was revealed by a patch of darkness where liquid resided. I'd read that at this stage the baby's head accounts for half of their total size. The scan backed this up and the circumference of their skull was greater than the length of their 6cm body.

Before arriving, we'd completed forms requesting the baby was screened for Down's, Edwards' and Patau's syndrome. In all three cases, babies with these disabilities have an extra chromosome. Unlike Down's syndrome, most babies with Edwards' or Patau's syndrome will die before or shortly after birth.

The screening for these disabilities is a combination of an ultrasound scan and a blood test. Sarah had carefully followed the advice in the original letter and made sure she didn't have an empty bladder at the time of the scan. Unfortunately, she'd been rather too successful in this regard, and her bladder was so full it caused the sonographer difficulties, requiring the scan to be briefly paused while Sarah found a cubicle. Once resumed, the sonographer was able to record measurements of the fluid at the back of the baby's neck to help calculate the likelihood of the baby having Down's, Edwards' or Patau's syndrome. Happily, the initial indications are the baby will test negative.

When the sonographer was finished, we were told the baby's due date was 15 May and were handed a set of images generated during the scan. Similar photos of friends' unborn children have always left me unmoved, but these precious pictures, I belatedly realised, are much like holiday snaps. They're uninteresting, unremarkable and, in some cases, downright unintelligible to anyone other than yourself (and possibly your mother).

During the second part of the appointment, Sarah's blood was taken and we had the chance to talk to a midwife. The cause of Sarah's positive antibody result remains a mystery, but we were again assured it's not significant. Likewise, when we admitted our error concerning the rare steak, we were told that as Sarah wasn't unwell after eating it, it was unlikely to have any health implications for the baby.

When we discussed the scan with our parents later that afternoon, our mums were both desperate to tell their friends about the pregnancy. We've asked them to hold tight a little longer until we receive the screening results.


**Day 89 - Saturday, 5 November**

Having driven down to west London to stay with our friends, Kat and Sean the night before, in the morning Sarah helped to make breakfast by stirring the coagulating scrambled eggs. She was soon overcome by nausea though and had to dash to the nearest bathroom. This, of course, is perfectly understandable. Particularly from my perspective, as I can't bear eggs. But it was amusing because Kat, who is 38 weeks pregnant, was cooking all the other components of a full English breakfast without a fuss.

Still, it gave us hope that Sarah's morning sickness won't last forever.

*Week 13*

## Day 91 - Monday, 7 November

The results are in. We received a letter in the post confirming our baby has a low chance of having Down's, Edwards' or Patau's syndrome. Specifically, we were informed the chance of the baby having Down's syndrome was precisely 1 in 1,591. The chance of the baby having either Edwards' or Patau's syndrome is considered even more remote at less than 1 in 10,000.

## Day 92 - Tuesday, 8 November

"Whatever you do, don't be overly apologetic or embarrassed," I insisted over breakfast. "Just tell him the facts so that he can plan accordingly."

"I know, but what am I going to say? 'Can I have a chat with you about...?'"

"You don't need to say what it's about. As long as you don't prevaricate, he'll understand pretty quickly where the conversation's going."

Sarah had been dreading this for weeks. Telling her boss - the founder and the only other employee at the charity where she worked - that she was pregnant. They were already juggling deadlines and it would not be the update he was looking for.

It seems neither Sarah's spate of hospital appointments nor her recent Covid jab had given the game away, for he wasn't expecting the news. When she arrived home, Sarah told me that he was happy for her, but was understandably concerned about the impact her absence would have.

## Day 94 - Thursday, 10 November

We have reserved our place on an antenatal course beginning in February. This is a little earlier than ideal as the
course is targeted at parents expecting babies between early
April and early May, but the course was a compromise
between the location, availability and times of the sessions.
Other courses ran for three six-hour sessions on successive
weekends and we were keen to avoid spending our final
three child-free Saturdays learning about birth.

Instead, we have signed up to a series of two-hour
sessions on weekday evenings. The course will be a good
opportunity to make new friends and we hope the atten-
dees' desire to avoid weekend courses is a sign they are like-
minded, outgoing individuals. Of course, it's best not to put
too much store in this. One friend recounted a fellow
mother-to-be asking their instructor if she knew of any sexy
swimsuits that were fitted with a flap to allow for easy access
during a water birth.

## Day 95 Friday, 11 November

This week is the first of Sarah's second trimester. Her pregnancy app says that during this stage Sarah will need to
increase her food intake by 300 calories per day (equivalent
to roughly three Kit Kats).

If Sarah's libido has increased, she hasn't told me.

## Day 96, Saturday 12 November

Little more than a week after the 12-week scan, I find myself
checking out nurseries. I wouldn't believe it if I wasn't living
it. Who have I become?

We're doing so because earlier in the week a pregnant

friend told us about the lack of available places in local nurseries. As we weren't intending to send our child to nursery for at least 14 months, we had been fairly relaxed about the issue. Besides, other friends had said the cost of sending a child to nursery was equivalent to a second mortgage, so we weren't even sure it would be financially feasible.

However, with her friend's warning ringing in her ears, Sarah was spurred into action and began shortlisting nurseries. When she phoned one, staff told her it was just as well she had as places were being reserved 18 months ahead of time. Presumably by people who haven't even conceived yet.

The nursery just so happened to have an open day today so we went to look around. As we walked there, we realised we had no idea of the type of questions we should be asking.

"So..." I said, imagining my imminent conversation with the nursery staff, "is the building structurally sound? Any asbestos in the ceiling?"

"I don't think they'd tell us if it did," Sarah pointed out. "Come on, we must be able to think of *something* worth asking."

Before we could come up with anything better, we arrived at the gates to the nursery. A couple pushing a toddler in a pram held the gate open for us. We walked up to the nursery together in awkward silence, until the child's mother asked the question Sarah and I had hoped she wouldn't.

"So how old is yours?"

"Err...they haven't arrived yet," Sarah said sheepishly. "We've been panicked into doing some research."

"Oh, ok! Well, Robbie really likes it here," she said, tousling the bowl-cut hair of her toddler as he looked up at us with curiosity.

We quickly realised the open day was not, as we had

assumed, for prospective parents interested in sending their children to the nursery. It was for parents whose children attended the nursery to see what they did all day. So we were very much the odd ones out.

After checking out the baby room, staff at the nursery encouraged us to look around the classrooms for the children aged two and above, but this felt too far into the future to imagine - even for us.


*Week 14*


### Day 98, Monday 14 November

Having checked out one local nursery, we feel obliged to visit another to compare it with. Like the first place we saw, it seems perfectly suitable. Admittedly, it's difficult to be assiduous though when the baby is the size of a kiwi fruit.


### Day 100, Wednesday 16 November

The pregnancy journey is measured by a multitude of milestones. Reaching a century of days is not one of them. But in the past few days Sarah has begun to 'show'. It's as if the baby was waiting until after the 12-week scan to reveal their presence. Clothes still conceal her bump, but when Sarah undresses the change is evident.

It's amazing to witness this natural progression. It's also quite amusing, for her previously slender stomach has been replaced by a little pot belly.

## Day 103, Saturday 19 November

Peter and his fiancee Katie pay us a visit and we spend the afternoon watching a Cambridge United match. The team are in League One, two divisions below the riches of the Premier League and unlikely to ever get there.

Yet I love the club. I never had a strong affiliation with a local team when I was growing up. Dad, a more casual football fan than I have ever been, allowed me to choose who I wanted to support. Like so many other boys in southern England in the 1990s, I opted for Manchester United. I was overjoyed when the club won the Treble, but as I grew up I had to accept I was simply a glory hunter who hadn't known any better.

Our son or daughter will avoid such a fate. I intend to do everything in my power to bring them up as a proud Cambridge supporter. This might represent a form of brainwashing, but it's only what Roman Catholics have been doing for generations.

## Day 104, Sunday 20 November

While following the River Cam back home from Grantchester, we decided we'll send the baby to the first nursery we visited, based on its proximity to our house. Quite how many days per week they'll be attending remains uncertain. Committing to full rather than half days comes with a discount, but I'm not sure we'll feel comfortable leaving a seven-month-old baby there for more than 10 hours per day.

Even with the reduced hourly rate, the costs rapidly add up. Childcare is more expensive in Britain than anywhere else in the developed world, amounting to more than half the earnings of the average parent according to a study in 2021 by the Organisation for Economic Co-operation and

Development. In most European countries this figure is well below 20%.

The Centre for Economic and Business Research estimates the total cost of raising a newborn baby to the age of 21 is £229,251. And no, this figure isn't inflated by private school fees. Needless to say, we won't be maximising our National Trust Family Life membership.

*Week 15*

### Day 105, Monday 21 November

This morning Sarah attended a routine midwife appointment and had her urine, blood pressure and carbon monoxide levels tested. I could have gone with her, but I had a fever. World Cup fever to be precise, for it was the day of England's opening match in Qatar.

### Day 106, Tuesday 22 November

According to Sarah's pregnancy apps, the baby's hairline is beginning to grow. Hopefully they'll take after Sarah, who in photos is comfortably the hairiest newborn baby I've ever seen. I was quite the opposite. Dad took one look at me and wanted to call me Winston. Thankfully he was overruled and my resemblance to the former British prime minister receded.

### Day 107, Wednesday 23 November

Two days after Sarah's appointment with the midwife, we received a letter summarising what was discussed. It informs us the baby will enjoy hearing Sarah sing and doing so will help the baby to "develop optimal brain growth in the womb as the stress hormone, cortisol, is lower." The midwife has clearly never heard Sarah sing.

## Day 108, Thursday 24 November

I've travelled north for a boys' week away in the Lake District. Sarah wasn't thrilled by the prospect, but we both know sauntering off on such trips might not be possible for much longer.

*Week 16*

## Day 114, Wednesday 30 November

The appearance of Sarah's stomach has altered in the days I've been away. Sarah's bump now begins higher up her torso, balancing out her short-lived pot belly.

I reached across to hold her as we lay in bed and noticed for the first time how gravity was pulling her stomach towards the mattress. Her burgeoning bump felt large in my right hand and I thought of our unborn child developing inside.

At least I did until curiosity got the better of me and I wondered what my own stomach felt like lying on my side. I realised, with some shame, that it felt much the same as Sarah's.

## Day 115, Thursday 1 December

Still reeling from last night's discovery, I stepped onto the scales and learned I've put on 15.5lb (7kg) since June. This is nearly double Sarah's own weight gain. Unlike Sarah, the only thing growing inside me is an accumulation of mince pies.

It's not uncommon for men to gain weight during their partner's pregnancy. Men who do so, or who experience other symptoms mimicking those of their expectant partners, such as stomach or back pain, are described as having Couvade syndrome. This is otherwise known as sympathetic pregnancy.

Some doctors consider the syndrome to be caused by hormonal changes, but many argue the condition is psychosomatic. While I'd like to believe my weight gain is a consequence of the deep empathy I feel for Sarah, I have a sneaking suspicion it might just be because I've turned into a couch potato.


**Day 117, Saturday 3 December**

Shortly before 12.45am at our final wedding of 2022, Sarah and I were taken aside by a new mother. Having learned Sarah was pregnant, she wanted to check Sarah would be receiving a 'push present'.

Our blank expressions suggested otherwise.

"Bitch, you deserve whatever you want," she declared. "Diamonds, a car, a handbag."

I laughed nervously but stopped when she fixed her eyes on me.

Speaking slowly and deliberately she said, "Her vagina is going to get ripped apart. If she wants a baby gem, you buy it for her. Whatever she wants, she gets."

I've told Sarah not to hold her breath.

## Day 118, Sunday 4 December

An Ipsos poll published today has found almost half of UK adults aged between 18 and 50 are not planning on having children. After recently learning how much it costs to raise them, I understand why.

In light of such statistics, it's little surprise the natural population of the UK is predicted to start declining within a few years.

At a time when pressure on pensions and the NHS is intensifying, it's good to know Sarah and I are doing our bit for the economy, if not for the planet.

*Week 17*

## Day 119, Monday 5 December

Sarah's nausea remains a constant, but the size of her stomach varies throughout the day. When she's getting dressed in the morning, it's easy to miss. Come evening, it's prominent.

One explanation for this is her bump expands as her abdominal muscles tire and relax over the course of the day. Another factor is that the bump may look larger when the baby is in a horizontal position in the womb. The most obvious explanation though is that the bump is bigger when it contains a stomach full of food. This explains why over the weekend Sarah received the most attention an hour after the hog roast at the wedding.

## Day 120, Tuesday 6 December

The baby is now the size of an orange - which is pretty impressive considering they were the size of an orange seed two and a half months ago.

Sarah's mum has admitted she's a little disappointed we haven't sent her weekly updates regarding the size of the baby. One of her friends has been receiving photos every week showing her expectant daughter and son-in-law holding fruit next to the bump to signify the baby's growth. This feels OTT, but writing this book means I'm in no position to judge.

## Day 121, Wednesday 7 December

While listening to Desert Island Discs, I learned John Legend curated the soundtrack to his wife's labour for the birth of their first child. This feels like another over the top gesture, but Sarah was surprisingly receptive to the idea. However, when it comes down to it, I doubt neither she, nor the midwives, will appreciate hearing *Push It!* by Salt-N-Pepa.

## Day 122, Thursday 8 December

Fetal flutters is the name given to the sensation of a baby's movements in the womb. They may be first experienced at any time between the 16th and 24th week of the pregnancy, but Sarah is already becoming impatient to feel them. If only to be reassured everything is ok.

"I thought I felt something the other day," Sarah said as we ate dinner. "But it might just have been wind."

"Eurgh! Tell me when you next think it's happening," I replied. "I'll make myself scarce."

## Day 123, Friday 9 December

I've learned our baby's heart is beating around 150 times per minute. This is twice the rate of an adult, but is already less than it was at its peak two months ago.

Sarah, meanwhile, is experiencing the latest unexpected side effect of pregnancy: a runny nose. Hormonal changes contribute to an increased production of mucus and cause approximately a third of women to have rhinitis at some stage of their pregnancy.

Of course, Sarah might just have a cold.

The sudden drop in temperature this week suggests it's the latter. The mercury hasn't risen much above freezing in recent days and Sarah gave me short shrift when I told her midwives recommend cold showers to relieve aches and pains.

I can't blame her. My heartbeat would rival the baby's if I was forced to take a cold shower at the moment.

*Week 18*

## Day 126, Monday 12 December

Having woken to a blanket of thick snow outside, Sarah decided against cycling into the office and worked from home instead. It was so cold in our house that by lunchtime she was wondering if she'd made the right decision.

"Why are my feet still so cold?" she asked me while perching on the radiator. "Can you Google 'Is it normal to get cold feet during pregnancy?'"

"I can," I replied hesitantly. "But I don't think you'll find the results very relevant. Or at least I hope you won't."

"Ok," she said, catching my drift. "Look up cold toes then."

It turns out cold feet are another side effect of the hormonal changes that occur during pregnancy.

Hormones certainly have a lot to answer for. Tonight Sarah cried at the farcical Lindsay Lohan film *Falling for Christmas*.


## Day 128, Wednesday 14 December

Sarah's bump remains concealed by the thick jumpers she wears around the house, but when she lies in bed, she looks like a Hollywood actress in the midst of preparations for a role requiring significant weight gain. Between her ribs and her pelvis, the former contours of her toned torso have been smoothed over and raised, like the snow cloaking the tiles on our roof.

While Sarah stoically takes each step as it comes, I remain captivated by the transformative effect of the pregnancy on her body. To my male brain, the unfolding evolutionary process is almost beyond comprehension.


## Day 129, Thursday 15 December

Two things happened today I never thought I'd see. Firstly, the Cam froze following days of sub-zero temperatures. Secondly, Sarah had to ask for my help to reach the top shelves of our cupboards.

"All of the ligaments in my stomach are really taut. I feel them stretching each time I raise my arms above my head," she explained.

I wasn't convinced stomach ligaments even existed, but, sure enough, they do.

Looks like I'll be responsible for changing light bulbs for the foreseeable future.

## Day 131, Saturday 17 December

Sarah navigated the rolling nationwide train strikes and travelled to London's South Bank for a friend's birthday. One of the five friends in attendance has a newborn and two others are expecting babies in the New Year. Afterwards, Sarah admitted to feeling envious that they have had the reassurance of receiving the all-clear at their 20-week scan.

The anxiety that marked the run-up to our 12-week scan has returned.

*Week 19*

## Day 133, Monday 19 December

Sarah is cross with me because I left the house having accidentally put the chocolate biscuits out of reach on the top shelf of the kitchen cupboard. Oops.

## Day 134, Tuesday 20 December

We're spending Christmas at Sarah's parents' house, where they live during the winter months. Their canal boat is an intimate place to go to the toilet at the best of times, but it feels positively routine in comparison to the current situation. Their house is one of thousands across the country without running water following the rapid thaw of frozen pipes. I'll never take flushing the toilet for granted again.

Still, things are looking up for Sarah. Just when we'd assumed she would have to forsake the collective gorging of turkey, mince pies and chocolates during the festive period, her nausea has abated and she has started to feel better. After 13 difficult weeks, it feels like a minor Christmas miracle.

## Day 135, Wednesday 21 December

It's dispiriting to think about, but whereas I used to count down the days until Christmas, I now look forward with equal excitement to the winter solstice. Or at least to its passing.

Today is not only the shortest day of the year, but officially the start of winter. A scary thought considering everywhere looked like Narnia last week. This halfway point of the solar calendar nearly coincides with the midway point of the pregnancy too.

At this stage, the baby's vernix caseosa is starting to develop. Vernix caseosa sounds like a spell from *Harry Potter*, but this name is preferable to its alternative: birthing custard. It describes the waxy, white substance that coats the skin of a newborn baby and protects them from pruning in the womb as a result of their prolonged contact with amniotic fluid.

## Day 136, Thursday 22 December

It was my turn to meet up with friends in London. Having not seen the three of them for six months, I was excited to tell them about Sarah's pregnancy. I was also pleased to be going somewhere that had flushing toilets.

"So when's it due?" one asked.

"Probably on one of your birthdays," I said to raised eyebrows. All three friends were born within nine days of 15 May.

"That's settled then. The baby's middle name should belong to whoever shares their birthday."

If we have a daughter, I doubt she'd thank me for that.

## Day 137, Friday 23 December

Sarah still hasn't felt any fetal flutters, but when I rubbed her bump like a genie's lamp this morning *I* felt something. I thought that if I was to detect anything, it would be a subtle movement across the length of my handspan as the baby stirred in the womb. Instead I felt a strong, isolated jab, akin to a punch or a kick.

"That was definitely something," I said, looking straight into Sarah's eyes. "What exactly, I don't know, but my body has definitely never done that before."

"It could be anything," Sarah reasoned before either of us got carried away. "My body is pretty different from yours right now."

"But could you not feel that inside you?"

"I don't think so."

Once again, I was astonished by the lack of sensation Sarah could feel given all of the activity happening inside her. I rubbed Sarah's stomach a few times more and received the same response. Each time the jab came from somewhere different.

"Maybe it is the baby, Sarah admitted hopefully. "But I might just have a twitchy tummy."

## Day 138, Christmas Eve, Saturday 24 December

Within 12 hours of suspecting her stomach muscles of spasming, Sarah's left leg went numb.

According to the NHS website, this is a symptom of a condition called Meralgia Paraesthetica. It's rarely anything serious or long lasting and is likely to be caused by Sarah's growing uterus pressing on nerves in her leg.

After going for a short walk, she felt pins and needles on the outside of her left thigh. Soon afterwards, she lost sensation there for more than an hour. At the start of the month Sarah and I had sandwiched the final wedding of the year between two tough hikes in Snowdonia. Now a walk in the park is, well, no longer a walk in the park.

Sarah is far from waddling though and all indications suggest she will 'carry small' throughout the pregnancy. Approaching 20 weeks, many expectant mothers have long since moved into maternity wear, but Sarah hasn't done so yet. Upon seeing her, friends joke that, given she used to have an almost concave stomach, it should be no surprise her bump is taking time to develop.

Sarah sleeps on her stomach (weird, I know) and all previous questions to midwives about when she should stop this to avoid restricting the baby's oxygen and blood supply have met with the same answer: "You'll know". Nevertheless, while it's easy to imagine women with large bumps not choosing to sleep on their front to avoid their head and feet floating in the air, we're sceptical Sarah will ever resemble a see-saw lying in bed this way.


### Day 139, Christmas Day, Sunday 25 December

I received a Cambridge United home shirt for Christmas and proudly wore it the rest of the day.

It feels odd to realise it's our last Christmas before we have a child. Over the past month, we've decorated the tree and watched the first snow of winter fall. Next year, we'll hopefully do so as a family and the magic of Christmas will be renewed.

I just hope the baby doesn't get all the presents.

*Week 20*

## Day 143, Thursday 29 December

We returned from the Christmas break to attend our 20-week scan in Cambridge. The appointment is also known by the scary name of the 'mid-pregnancy anomaly scan', as the sonographer conducting the scan searches for any anomalies that may affect the baby's health and development.

The baby's growth over the past two months was evident immediately. Their appearance made the images printed at the 12-week scan look like they were of a germinating runner bean. I spent much of the scan saying "wow", although I'm unsure whether this was in response to seeing our baby on-screen, or simply awe at the technology that enables it.

The sonographer showed us the four ventricles of the heart and used software to detect the flow of blood around the uterus. When she turned her attention to the baby's spine, the sharp contrast of the baby's skeletal structure made them look like a dinosaur fossil.

The sonographer would go several minutes without uttering a word while completing various measurements. Each time it was difficult not to fear the worst.

Many parents choose to find out the gender of their baby at the 20-week scan. We decided not to.

It's a rare example where, for people such as ourselves, scientific progress has outstripped the appetite for knowledge. Friends have found our desire to remain in the dark bizarre and have questioned how we'll prepare for the newborn. Moreover, I've detected an element of dismay when discussing our decision not to know with the parents of older children. I can't decide whether this is due to their reluctance to indulge in what they perceive to be a foolish pursuit, or simply disappointment that by keeping it a surprise we've deprived them of imparting, at great length, advice on how to raise a girl or boy.

Conveniently, our baby was lying with their legs close together during the scan. I tried not to look, but as I didn't spot anything, I'm counting this as evidence she's a girl.

The sonographer seemed disappointed not to be part of the big reveal, but hopefully the midwives will be pleased.

Of course, not knowing increases the speculation. A secret Chinese gender predictor graph developed in the 17th century was reportedly used by the imperial family. By considering the mother's age and the month when the baby is conceived, the graph claims to be 90% accurate.

It predicts we will have a boy, but Mum shared my scepticism about the graph, pointing out that it was easy to boast a 90% success rate given the Qing dynasty's track record of abandoning newborn daughters in the forest.

After nearly an hour we were given the all-clear and told the baby's estimated measurements. Overall, they are in the 48th percentile, with a similar-sized head. Their legs and stomach are more noteworthy, having been calculated to be in the 28th and 83rd percentile respectively. Sarah and I have athletic builds and an average height of more than 6ft, so we laughed out loud when told of the baby's dimensions. Let's hope they like sumo wrestling.

**Day 145, New Year's Eve, Saturday 31 December**

Sarah and I hosted a small party to see in 2023. We both feel excited and a little apprehensive about the year ahead.

As the clock struck midnight I turned to give Sarah a kiss. "Five and a half months until you're on maternity leave," I said.

"Four and a half you mean?"

"Do I? Oh yes."

New Year's resolution number one: learn to count. Otherwise, there's no chance I'll be ready for the baby.

## Day 146, New Year's Day, Sunday 1 January

Mum sends Sarah and I a link to an article in *The Times*. It concerns a study in Australia suggesting that women find it easier to lose weight after giving birth if their partner is fully involved in parenting.

That'll be New Year's resolution number two, then.

*Week 21*

## Day 147, Monday 2 January

We spent the first Bank Holiday of the year shopping. I'm hoping it doesn't set a precedent.

I've begun to notice things I didn't used to. For example, on a packet of Duracell batteries, I spotted a picture of a crying baby's face with the words 'repulsive taste'. There can't be many products with such a selling point.

Intrigued, I bought the batteries and, upon returning home, gave them a lick. Duracell won't be falling foul of the advertising regulator, that's for sure.

## Day 148, Tuesday 3 January

In recent days the baby has appeared particularly active when Sarah first lies down in bed. This pattern has belatedly convinced Sarah it wasn't her abdominal muscles twitching after all.

## Day 150, Thursday 5 January

We saw the baby moving for the first time tonight. Each time the baby kicked or punched, the skin directly above the activity rose, as if a tiny tent pole had been briefly erected in Sarah's abdomen.

## Day 151, Friday 6 January

Tonight when we went to bed, the baby wasn't as active as before. I wasn't unduly perturbed as Sarah had felt them move a few hours earlier and it seems unfair to expect them to behave like a performing monkey. The lack of internal karate kicks worried Sarah though. Particularly when she read on the NHS website that we should call the maternity unit if:

- your baby is moving less than usual
- you cannot feel your baby moving any more
- there is a change to your baby's usual pattern of movements

The website urged expectant mothers not to 'wait until the next day - call immediately, even if it's the middle of the night.'

I'm still better at sensing the baby's movements than Sarah, so I rubbed her stomach hoping to elicit a response. I didn't get one. Unlike the night before, the only activity I could detect corresponded with normal digestion.

It was late so, in spite of the official guidance, we went to sleep, hoping for the best.

## Day 152, Saturday 7 January

Much to our relief, Sarah felt the baby kicking again on the drive down to London to see Kat and Sean. Since we last saw them, Kat has given birth to a baby boy who is now six weeks old.

Watching them, tired but already seamlessly adapting to Max's arrival, it was strange to think that our own child - whose presence is still entirely concealed under a jumper - will one day be in the same school year as Max. It's even stranger to think that, many years from now, they'll be part of the class of '41.

*Week 22*

## Day 154, Monday 9 January

"The baby went crazy this afternoon," Sarah told me while chopping vegetables in the kitchen. "It felt like they were trying out wrestling moves."

"Perhaps they were making up for a quiet night on Friday?"

"Maybe. I had to Google whether a baby can move *too* much."

"And can it?"

"Apparently not."

That morning Sarah had attended a pregnancy pilates class, which may have had something to do with the baby's somersaults later in the day. The class aimed to help expectant mothers adapt to their changing bodies. The teacher doubted whether Sarah was actually pregnant, but Sarah found the class, and specifically the exercises targeting her pelvic floor, beneficial.

"Just be careful you don't overdo it," she was warned. "Pelvic floor muscles loosen during pregnancy due to changes in your hormones. Strengthening them excessively won't help the birth."

Which is the last thing you need if you're giving birth to The Rock.

## Day 155, Tuesday 10 January

Sarah has bought a pregnancy pillow. Shaped like a human-sized banana, it's designed to support Sarah's bump and hips at night.

"It's huge!" I said to Sarah as I watched her unpack it. "Is there going to be any room for me in bed?"

"Yes, it'll be fine. Believe me, this is one of the less obtrusive ones."

I didn't believe her until I looked online and found an assortment of enormous, curiously shaped alternatives. They're more like giant soft pods to sleep inside than pillows. At a time when couples are encouraged to foster intimacy, there are few more effective ways to do the opposite than have one person cocoon themselves in soft furnishings that take up almost the entirety of the bed.

## Day 156, Wednesday 11 January

It might not be one of the biggest pregnancy pillows on the market, but the bed still felt smaller last night. I woke early to find Sarah clutching the pillow and, feeling like a spare part, decided to get up. Biologically, I guess I've already played my part.

## Day 157, Thursday 12 January

Another poor night's sleep. This time the pregnancy pillow wasn't to blame, but the person cuddling it. Sarah has started to snore.

"It's not my fault! It's the baby," Sarah protested as we lay in bed the following morning.

I suspected our baby was being used as a scapegoat, and insinuated as much. But once again, science backed Sarah up. Pregnant women do snore more. This is because high levels of oestrogen and progesterone cause the mucus membranes in the nose to swell.

Even more reason then to encourage Sarah to sleep on her side.

## Day 160, Sunday 15 January

We marked reaching four months until the due date by taking the first photo of Sarah's bump. Delightful though the image is, we managed to refrain from posting it on social media.

### Week 23

## Day 162, Tuesday 17 January

We had deliberately waited until after the 20-week scan before beginning the daunting task of shopping for the baby. We started by attending a free 'baby appointment' at John Lewis. I'm aware of how middle class this sounds, but we'd been recommended to go to gain an understanding of the products available. Equipped with this knowledge we could then search Facebook Marketplace for parents desperate to get rid of the stuff.

We began by looking at prams, which all looked much the same: sturdy, elaborate chariots that were unlikely to fit in the back of our Toyota Aygo. Trying shoes on in a shop often makes me feel self-conscious, but it was nothing compared to steering an empty pram around a department store to test its manoeuvrability.

While prams are notoriously expensive, we hadn't anticipated the cost and variety of types of car seats. It's now a legal requirement for children to use a car seat until they're 12 years old or 135cm (4'4) tall. Buying them secondhand (car seats, not children) is discouraged, in case they have been dropped or involved in a car accident.

Many seats only fit babies until they are approximately nine months old. To try to get some value for money (a difficult feat for something that costs up to £300), we focused on getting a seat that could be used until the baby was four years old. Some models can be adapted all the way until they are 12, but they require so much padding a newborn baby would almost disappear inside them. Picturing the effect a decade of spilt drinks and vomit would have also made these seats less desirable.

Given the lack of space in our car, we began to appreciate the potential benefits of buying a 360° swivel base. This enables parents to put the baby's seatbelt on without the adult needing to fold their body like origami.

It's a slippery slope though. In an industry where every problem has a product that claims to offer a solution, it's easy to get carried away.

An hour into the session, I began to feel overwhelmed. It's no wonder some prospective parents fork out £1,500 on a complete travel system to minimise the time spent shopping. Fortunately, I was able to zone out entirely when we were shown the hi-tech gadgets. We won't be needing baby monitors which measure air humidity. Neither will we be needing monitors capable of pre-recording bedtime stories, nor ones that send notifications to your phone such as 'Mom, I fell asleep 15 minutes ago'.

Many of the products seemed superfluous or even vulgar. Whether it's push presents, baby showers or absurdly expensive baby clothes, the naked commercialism behind it all is hard to ignore.


## Day 164, Thursday 19 January

Following our trip to John Lewis, Sarah found a Moses basket going free on Facebook Marketplace. I wasn't sure what a Moses basket was, but not wanting to look a gift horse in the mouth, I agreed to pick it up.

It looks ok, but smells strongly of chicken tikka masala. Hopefully the baby won't mind.


## Day 166, Saturday 21 January

We're on a roll. Sarah spotted someone on Facebook was selling a secondhand baby sling so we swooped in to collect it. As part of the deal the woman gave us several heavy boxes of maternity, baby and infant clothes for free. We picked up a high chair and a baby bath too. The seller was happy to wash her hands of it all and we were grateful for her generosity. Our car's suspension was less appreciative.


## Day 167, Sunday 22 January

I swallowed two tablets of sodium valproate this morning, as I have done every morning for nearly two decades to control my epilepsy.

For several years pregnant women have been advised not to take the drug as sodium valproate causes deformities to 10% of babies exposed to it in the womb. The failure to prevent the thousands of cases that have occurred has been compared to the thalidomide scandal of the 1960s, which is estimated to have caused 10,000 miscarriages, stillbirths and infant deaths in the UK alone.

I'd asked doctors about the health implications of continuing to take sodium valproate, but had always been told there was no reason to worry as the birth defects were exclusively associated with women who had been prescribed the drug.

The latest evidence suggests otherwise. Today it was reported in *The Sunday Times* 'there are emerging risks to male sperm from sodium valproate as well as fertility issues'. I'm one of 100,000 men in the UK of child-bearing age currently taking the drug. Under the new rules being introduced, patients should have their prescriptions reviewed by two doctors and be switched to an alternative where possible.

This news comes too late for our baby.


*Week 24*


**Day 169, Tuesday 24 January**

I was cleaning my teeth when Sarah pointed out her linea nigra for the first time. It's faint, but it's an unmistakable vertical line that runs from her belly button to her pubic area. The line is caused by, you guessed it, an increase in pregnancy hormones and usually fades away after birth.

While looking at the line, we both remarked how much her stomach has grown in recent days. This coincides with the start of an anticipated growth spurt for the baby, which will see them double in weight over the next four weeks.

## Day 171, Thursday 26 January

I was at home when Sarah called. She'd left the house half an hour earlier and I could immediately hear she was upset.

"Hey, I just wanted to ask–"

"–Are you ok? What's wrong?"

"I'm fine, but I fell off my bike on the way to work."

"Are you sure you're ok? Where are you now?"

"Yes, I think so. It was such a stupid little mistake - I slipped on the wet surface. I've just arrived at the office."

"How did you land?

"On my side."

"I think you should call the midwives."

"That's what I was going to ask. Do you think it's necessary? I feel fine, just a bit shaken up. My bike's handlebars need a bit of realigning, but other than that..."

This suggested her accident was worse than Sarah was letting on. "Do you want me to come and pick you up?"

"No, it's fine."

"How does the baby feel?"

"I don't know. Hopefully ok. I think I've felt them move once since I got back up."

The midwives reassured Sarah over the phone that the baby is well protected. They said unless she notices any changes, such as if the baby stops moving, she shouldn't worry.

However, it's difficult not to worry when you're expecting and this incident, combined with the change in guidance about my medication, makes it harder than ever.

## Day 173, Saturday 28 January

Sarah normally takes the lead when assembling flat-pack furniture and I've always taken for granted her willingness to assist with traditionally masculine chores.

Heavy lifting isn't a good idea during pregnancy though.

After spending the day assembling wardrobes and ferrying unwanted bulky items to charity shops, I began to appreciate how fortunate I am not to have signed up to this role for a lifetime.

## Day 174, Sunday 29 January

The preventable smashing of a brand new mirror has led to the first citing of 'pregnancy brain' in our house. Just a few hours later, Sarah fell over an innocuous section of pavement. It feels like we're entering a new phase of the pregnancy.

A study in the *Maternal and Child Health Journal* found 27% of pregnant women suffer a fall during pregnancy, and, according to the University of Cincinnati, nearly two-thirds of these occur during the second trimester. One reason for this is that while a woman's centre of gravity is shifting forwards every day, her brain is still using pre-bump muscle memory. Further hindering her chances of staying upright is the body's increased production of the hormone relaxin, which not only relaxes ligaments in the pelvis ready for childbirth, but other ligaments too.

And I thought I had it tough trying not to look clumsy as a teenager.

*Week 25*

## Day 175, Monday 30 January

Sarah kicked off the week with a scheduled appointment with the midwife, who calculated the size of her bump. There are no scans at these interim appointments, so the size is estimated by running a tape measure between the highest point of Sarah's uterus and her pubic bone.

At 25 weeks, pregnant women are expected to have a 25cm bump. Those with a bump greater than 27cm, or less than 23cm, are recommended to have additional scans to make sure everything is ok.

A week ago, we'd predicted that we would be paying the sonographer a visit. So we were pleased to learn Sarah's bump is within the permitted range.

Her height has been helping to hide it all along.

## Day 177, Wednesday 1 February

The baby has begun to form their first memories, which is why parents are encouraged to talk to them and play soothing music they'll recognise outside of the womb. While some parents are no doubt providing a constant stream of classical music (the benefits of which remain open to debate), our less highbrow tastes mean the baby is listening to Madonna rather than Mozart.

The baby also has 1,000 ligaments now and all 33 vertebrae in their spine. Until this week though, their nostrils hadn't begun to open, leading me to imagine that Sarah has been carrying a miniature Lord Voldemort.

## Day 179, Friday 3 February

I spent my Friday night driving around Cambridgeshire picking up secondhand baby paraphernalia. How has it come to this?

One of the items I collected was a free cot bed. The owners offered to give us the mattress, but we decided to splash out on a new one. At least that won't smell like an Indian restaurant.


## Day 180, Saturday 4 February

Sarah has spent recent days scouring Facebook Marketplace for a pram. After being beaten to the punch several times by rival bargain hunters, Sarah followed the advice of a pregnant friend who suggested she extended her location radius beyond Cambridge, to include areas where our parents live. The baby may not be born yet, but that wasn't going to prevent us from calling in an early favour.

It was my parents that drew the short straw. Luckily, the owner of the pram, a man named James, was willing to drive 40 minutes to their house to drop it off. He almost certainly hadn't anticipated that Mum would insist he demonstrated the many ways the Uppababy Vista pram and its accessories could be configured and disassembled.

Halfway through Mum's recording of James' awkward instructional videos, he must have realised there were easier ways to get £80.


## Day 181, Sunday 5 February

It was the kind of beautiful sunny day that lulls you into believing spring is just around the corner. So we put down our brushes, jumped on our bikes and escaped the smell of fresh paint pervading through the house.

We hadn't visited the nearby Gog Magog Hills for years and, upon arriving, quickly went astray. We ended up surrounded by inquisitive canines in the dog play area. Most lost interest when they realised we possessed neither toys nor treats, but one cavapoo remained steadfastly by our side.

"Molly! Molly, come here," her owner beckoned.

In spite of our efforts to encourage Molly to return to her owner, she ignored him.

"Molly! Molly!" he continued in vain. "Looks like you've got a friend for life," he said, giving up as he walked towards her, lead in hand.

We walked on, buoyed by the encounter. "I like the name Molly," Sarah said.

"Me too. It's a good name for a dog. Not one I'd choose for our daughter though."

"No."

The subject was left hanging in the air. We had been putting off selecting the baby's name for months. Couples rarely have the same first choice, so the decision almost inevitably involves compromise. It's one thing to yield to your partner's preferences when buying varieties of apple, but quite another to give them free rein to the name of your child. You don't want to end up with a name you later regret.

After taking a few strides, Sarah grasped the nettle. "What *are* we going to call the baby if it's a girl?"

"Erm...I dunno."

"I like Thea."

"Thea?"

"Yeah."

"That's not a name."

"It is!"

"Well it's not the name of our daughter."

"Fine," Sarah persisted. "What about Paige?"

"That's something you write on. I'm vetoing that too."

"Ok, well you suggest some names then."

"How about...Anna?"

"Anna Atkin?"

"Yeah."

"No, we can't go alliterative. The poor girl's initials would be the same as Alcoholics Anonymous."

"It feels a bit nuclear vetoing all names beginning with A. No Alice, Amy or Anita then."

"Were you planning on calling our daughter Anita?"

"Probably not. So no A's," I said, admiring the snowdrops by the edge of the path. "How about Hannah? It's easy to spell."

"No - I didn't like a Hannah I went to school with."

"What about Jess?"

"No. My cousin's called Jess."

"This game might be tricky if we're ruling out every relative, friend and acquaintance we've ever met."

"Let's keep trying."

"I like Olivia," I offered.

"So do I, but Olivia has been the most popular name in England for years. There'll be three other Olivias in her class."

"But ours will be the best. What about...Sienna?"

"That's rogue."

"Yeah, that was my thinking. How many Siennas do you know?"

"None. Do you know any?"

"Only Miller - the actress. But we're not exactly close."

"The problem with Sienna is she will have the same initials as me," Sarah pointed out. "You've always said it's not ideal sharing initials with your mum."

"True. She always accidentally opened my post."

"Maybe we spell Sienna with a C?"

"No, that's my initial instead."

"Ha! Of course. We could use a silent P. The teachers would hate that. 'No Miss, it's Psienna - the P is silent like in psychology.'"

I laughed. "I'm sure our daughter would always be grateful we inflicted a lifetime of administrative difficulties on them."

"Yes, maybe Sienna isn't the right first name. It could be a fun middle name though," Sarah said.

In recent weeks we had both used the baby naming app Kinder, which matches names you and your partner have independently shortlisted. As we walked, I looked at the list for inspiration.

"How about Zoe?"

"Zoe Sienna Atkin," Sarah said, trying it out.

"That girl's got something about her. She's no plain Jane. I like it," I said. "But I still like Olivia. Olivia..."

"–Rose?"

"Olivia Rose is nice too."

"How should we choose?" Sarah asked, slipping her hand into my coat pocket.

"We could wait and see on the day whether they look like an Olivia or a Zoe?"

"I've never seen a baby and thought that's an Olivia - or a Zoe."

"That's because you haven't seen *our* Zoe."

"Perhaps," said Sarah, sounding unconvinced. "Let's see how we feel in a few days' time."

We had already agreed to call the baby James if they're a boy. While we're grateful for the pram, we haven't deliberately chosen to name the baby after the pram's previous owner. Deciding on a middle name has proved harder than anticipated though, so if we're still struggling we might ask him for his.

## Week 26

### Day 182, Monday 6 February

This evening we were added to a Whatsapp group featuring everyone who'll be attending our antenatal classes. Obviously, you shouldn't judge a person by their WhatsApp picture. But I do. Particularly the person whose picture is of their 20-week scan. At least I assume it's *their* 20-week scan...

### Day 183, Tuesday 7 February

Before we rule out any more names for our baby, Sarah has gone online in search of inspiration. Her Facebook feed is now full of articles with ridiculous titles such as '16 Gorgeous Baby Boy Names That End In 'E'' and '25 Futuristic Baby Names That Are Actually Gorgeous'. There is also the downright tragic 'Baby Names With The Highest Earning Potential' and '100 Ugly Girl Names And Ugly Boy Names You'd Want To Avoid'. The headlines are supposed to serve as click bait, but have completely the opposite effect. However, I couldn't resist clicking on a *Daily Mirror* article with the headline 'Woman Shares Name She Really Wants To Give Daughter But Can't As It's A Bacteria'. Fortunately, Salmonella was never in the running for us.

I did some background checks myself by Googling whether there are any serial killers called James or Olivia Atkin. As far as I can tell, there aren't, but Zoe Atkin is a British freestyle skier.

This means our theoretical daughter would not be the

first Zoe Atkin to feature at the Winter Olympics. Which is a shame, but not a dealbreaker.

## Day 184, Wednesday 8 February

Tonight we attended our first antenatal class. Traditionally, many of these courses have been run by the National Childbirth Trust (NCT), but ours is run by a popular competitor called Bump and Baby. I've jokingly referred to the organisation as Bump and Grind so many times since we signed up in November that the new name has stuck.

It's similar to when Dad secretly changed the name of the 'Fax & Send' desktop icon on our family computer to 'Fax & Sex', leading me to presume that was what the application was called until an embarrassing incident at school.

This time, I've no one to blame but myself.

After a couple of introductory games, the session focused on labour and childbirth. While creating variously dilated cervixes out of Play-Doh, I lost track of how to count contractions. Worse still, we were the only couple who failed to replicate birth by not managing to pop a table tennis ball out of a balloon. In two weeks' time we'll be back for the second lesson on childbirth, where we'll be discussing assisted deliveries.

Hopefully we'll do better next time round. I'll try to avoid wincing so much for a start.

## Day 185, Thursday 9 February

Now we've commenced our antenatal course, everything is starting to feel much more imminent. Occasionally, moments of excitement give way to a sense of apprehension. I've no doubt the good bits of having a baby are great and that seeing them smile and learning to talk will be thrilling.

But even after accepting neither will happen for some time, I can't shake off the suspicion that such moments will make up only a fraction of our day-to-day existence and the majority will be spent doing simple things, such as leaving the house, that we used to do without thinking.

I've heard new parents describe the first year after the birth of their child as the best of their lives. I want to believe them. I'm just not sure I do.

## Day 186, Friday 10 February

"Look at this," Sarah said, lifting up her top as she lay on the sofa.

We've gradually become accustomed to her bump, but neither of us had seen it look like this before. The baby had adopted a position that made Sarah's stomach bulge to one side, making it look like it belonged to an anaconda that's swallowed a deer.

Sarah has been struggling to sleep all week and, looking at this, I'm not surprised she's felt uncomfortable. It's a cruel trick of nature to make it so difficult to rest when you know that getting eight hours of sleep per night will soon be a thing of the past.

## Day 187, Saturday 11 February

At this stage of their development, more than half of the baby's energy is dedicated to growing their brain. This week marks the point at which their eyelids open for the first time too.

## Week 27

### Day 190, Tuesday 14 February

Sarah went to the doctors for another routine appointment to have her blood levels checked. While she was out I hastily scribbled a limerick in a handmade Valentine's Day card. It read:

> There once was a pregnant girl,
> Who felt like she needed to hurl
> She was told to take it easy,
> To save her feeling queasy
> But it's hard when spring begins to unfurl

I kept the card anonymous.

In spite of the poem's poor wordplay, that evening we made the most of our last child-free Valentine's Day.

"Does it bother you having sex when I'm this pregnant?" Sarah asked afterwards.

"Not at all. If it was going to trouble me, I think it would have done so before now."

"Some men don't like it though, do they?"

"Apparently not. I can understand why, but I've read enough health websites to believe it when they say that no matter how much my ego might try to convince me otherwise, I'm not big enough to upset the baby. As long as we're sensible, the baby is perfectly protected in there. Besides, I wasn't going to go four months before the birth without sex - and abstain for three days after - just because I wasn't feeling it."

"Three days, you reckon?" Sarah laughed.

It's good to start the post-partum negotiations early.

**Day 191, Wednesday 15 February**

"It's amazing to think we'll have a baby three months from now," I said as I took a photo of Sarah standing in profile.

"People keep telling me how fast the time will go," Sarah replied. "I'm sure they're right, but 12 weeks feels like a long time to be getting bigger and more uncomfortable every day."

I reached across and put my hand on Sarah's bare stomach. I sympathised. Her skin already feels as tight as a drum.


**Day 192, Thursday 16 February**

Lying in bed at the end of the day, Sarah's stomach rose and fell conspicuously as the baby changed position. It was like watching a rug move as a mouse ran underneath it.

Now we're at 27 weeks, the baby is apparently sleeping and waking at regular intervals. They don't seem to have chosen the most convenient schedule, for Sarah still sleeps fitfully.


**Day 194, Saturday 18 February**

I spent the afternoon planning our summer holiday to Northern Ireland, where we'll be attending Nana's funeral. To be clear, the funeral has been delayed - we're not crossing the Irish Sea to commit murder.

We hope to go hiking in the Mourne Mountains while we're there in July, but accept that our usual 15+ mile hikes may be too long for Sarah so soon after the birth. I decide we'll aim for 10-milers instead.

## Day 195, Sunday 19 February

Sarah has returned from a weekend in London, where she was introduced to her friends' newborn babies. She walked through the door with far more than she left.

"What's all this?" I asked, taking the bags from her.

"It's stuff from my friends. They've given us loads of things - a birthing ball, nappies, maternity pads–"

"What, like nipple pads?"

"No, for when my vagina is leaking blood after the birth."

"Oh, right."

Things are getting very real very quickly.

*Week 28*

## Day 196, Monday 20 February

Today represented a genuine, medically-recognised landmark in the pregnancy journey: the start of the third trimester. At this point, mothers-to-be are encouraged to raise their calorie intake by an additional 150 calories, so that, when added to the second trimester increase, they are consuming 450 calories (the equivalent of roughly two Mars bars) more per day than they did pre-pregnancy.

All the guidance emphasises that, contrary to popular belief about 'eating for two', women should not eat twice as much as before as this would only worsen their health. This makes sense, but it would have disappointed me immensely if I was carrying our child.

I've taken small steps towards losing the weight I've gained since the conception, but Sarah's increased appetite has made it harder to resist temptation.

## Day 197, Shrove Tuesday, 21 February

Sarah's tummy button has turned as flat as the pancakes we had for dessert. As is generally the case, its appearance had always previously been partially concealed. Now it has come to the surface, the wrinkles make it look like a dried up jellyfish.

As she got into bed and allowed her head to sink into the pillow, Sarah let out a long sigh.

"The third trimester isn't much fun. I couldn't understand why everyone says the second trimester is so good, but it's better than this." She stared up at the ceiling. "I just feel big and uncomfortable. And I'm not nearly as big as most of the girls at our antenatal class. How do people move when they get bigger than this?"

"I don't know," I said, looking enviously at the space afforded to the pregnancy pillow and wondering if I could distract Sarah with flattery to take possession of a third of the bed. "You're doing very well."

Sarah refuted this and didn't budge an inch.


## Day 198, Ash Wednesday, 22 February

At our second antenatal class I was the guinea pig for the group and was asked to portray a mother giving birth during a caesarean. It turned out to be a surprisingly good gig, as I spent a lot of the class on my back. I could see very little as other volunteers replicated the surgery by lifting a sheet above my chest. It was too much for one of the dads-to-be; he later admitted that while holding up the towel to conceal the imagined surgery he began to feel faint at the idea of it all. He had to sit down and have his heavily pregnant wife stand in for him.

My performance may have been worthy of an Oscar, but

my mind began to drift. *Why is it called a caesarean?* Subsequent research indicated although a legend exists that Julius Caesar was born this way and the procedure was named after him, it's more likely the term comes from the Latin *caedere*, meaning to cut.

Anyway, my main take away from the class was that I wouldn't want to have a caesarean. The other revelations were:

1) An instrumental birth didn't, disappointingly, refer to having an orchestra present to announce the arrival of the baby.

2) After giving birth to the baby, the mother must give birth to the placenta. Which, at approximately 22cm in diameter, is considerably larger than either Sarah or I had imagined.

3) New mothers will need to wear maternity nappies for about a week and are likely to continue bleeding for another five weeks after that. This suggests my plans for 10-mile walks in Northern Ireland six weeks after the birth may be a tad ambitious.

4) Epidurals can be almost entirely effective at eliminating pain, but are not without risks and so some women choose to avoid them. They can be associated with a drop in blood pressure, can affect a woman's ability to move around during labour and in certain circumstances may increase the chance of needing additional support during the delivery.

I'd be inclined not to have an epidural, but it's irrelevant what my pain-free body thinks would be best. It's Sarah's decision and if she chooses to up the ante with the pain relief I'm not going to counsel otherwise. If she's really out of it, she might not even notice the saxophonist I've snuck into the delivery room.

## Day 199, Thursday 23 February

While attending a scheduled appointment with a midwife, Sarah asked about her recent blood results, some of which were a fraction below the defined healthy parameters. The midwife reassured Sarah they weren't a cause for concern as the guidelines were based on male physiology. Assuming this is true, it's absurd. Why in the 21st century are we still using men as the benchmark for pregnant women?

As always, the midwife was keen to know if Sarah was regularly feeling the baby move. Much of the time Sarah finds it difficult to judge the extent of the baby's movements, which I still find hard to comprehend. I'm confident I'd be able to feel something the size of a pineapple moving inside *my* abdomen. But as Sarah pointed out, it's similar to being asked how many times a sore cut hurts. At the end of each day you don't know how many times it did - you just know the cut is there.

## Day 200, Friday 24 February

The end of the working week brought up Sarah's double century. The modest pot belly Sarah had 100 days ago now seems a distant memory.

The 200th day of the pregnancy happened to correspond with the date of our 28-week scan. This was the first of two additional scans we were asked to attend as part of a medical research study into the cause of pregnancy complications. We'd been told little information about the baby's development would be shared with us at these scans, but it was still reassuring to learn that everything looked ok.

The baby was sitting upright in Sarah's womb, which sounds like good news, except for the fact that, ideally, they will be born head-first. It's only a cause for slight concern if the baby hasn't moved from its current breech position by the time of our next research scan at 36 weeks. If they haven't, it makes it more likely that the doctors will recommend Sarah has a caesarean.

On the way home we picked up a secondhand nappy bin and a microwaveable steriliser for £5. We haven't yet worked out how to use the nappy bin - Sarah didn't take me up on my offer to test it - but it's designed to individually encase each soiled nappy in a bag to contain the smell and then string them together like sausages.

An image as intriguing as it is disgusting.


## Day 201, Saturday 25 February

My parents visited us in Cambridge, bringing with them our newly purchased, nine-year-old pram. It's bigger than I'd anticipated, with rear wheels the diameter of basketballs.

Even with the benefit of James' videos, folding it up was far from straightforward. We got the hang of it eventually, but only after Sarah had narrowly avoided taking Dad's legs out from under him.


## Day 202, Sunday 26 February

Sarah told me she intended to write a list of items (pre-owned or otherwise) that we needed to buy before the baby's arrival. I left her to it and when I walked back in from the garden an hour later, she was kneeling upside down against the sofa.

"What are you doing?"

"It's called the Forward Leaning Inversion."

"Right."

"It's supposed to provide a bit of extra space in my uterus and encourage the baby to go head-first," Sarah explained.

I took up the same position beside Sarah and soon felt lightheaded. I didn't feel much better after taking a look through Sarah's list. She had tried to keep it as manageable as possible, but it was still intimidatingly long and featured everything from muslins to nipple cream.

*Week 29*

**Day 203, Monday 27 February**

I booked the ferry to Northern Ireland this evening. The only problem was when the form asked for the name and gender of our baby. I panicked, selected female and gave her name as TBC.

I must avoid being in this position when registering the birth.

**Day 204, Tuesday 28 February**

While running along the Cam on a blustery grey day, I reflected on how my behaviour as a father-to-be already differs from what I'd predicted. In my twenties I'd imagined I would commit time every day to enhancing our baby's early development to give it the best possible chance in life. But so far I've felt no inclination to play foreign language podcasts next to Sarah's womb. For that, Sarah is grateful, yet she remains unconvinced by the strength of her own maternal instinct.

Looking at our peers, it's easy to identify parents who have become defined by their baby. I'm determined to avoid this. Sarah and I are not so deluded as to believe that our existing lifestyle won't be impacted by caring for the baby, but we want to try to retain a sense of ourselves. Some might argue this reveals either a profound level of naivety or an unwillingness to fully support our child. Or possibly both.

I prefer to think it shows a desire to raise a baby that's healthy and happy, rather than a polyglot.

## Day 206, Thursday 2 March

So far, much of the antenatal course had been about the birth itself, where my role would be relatively minimal. Tonight we learned about the day-to-day chores of raising a child. First we were asked to place nappies with different colour faeces in order of development. Even though I knew for the purposes of the demonstration meconium (the substance of the baby's first poo) consisted of Marmite and that pesto and baby food substituted for the later stools, I still found the idea of changing the nappies unpleasant and I'm sceptical I'll grow to become blase about changing nappies in the way many parents do.

Our instructor showed us some photos of a baby with an extremely dirty nappy. The scene was so catastrophic I had to openly admit I had no idea what I was looking at. The poo had exploded up the baby's back, down its legs and turned every inch of the baby's nappy mustard yellow. While I'd hoped such poonamis were mythical events, I was at least aware they might be possible. There were other topics I knew nothing about. For example, we learned the nappies of baby girls may contain a little blood during the first few days of their lives. This is called pseudomenstruation and happens because the baby is no longer receiving oestrogen from their mother's placenta.

If we're having a girl, I have an awful lot to learn.

**Day 209, Sunday 5 March**

I can't see Sarah undress without laughing any more. Her torso is now completely different to its pre-pregnancy shape. She's good enough to tolerate my mirth because she knows that although I'm laughing at her, rather than with her, I find her comical curves seductive.

*Week 30*

**Day 210, Monday 6 March**

We're three quarters of the way there. The baby is now about 40cm long and weighs roughly 2lb 14oz (1.3kg). Over the past week they've become chubbier, which will make it easier for them to regulate their body temperature at birth. The development of this layer of fat is the catalyst for the soft, fine hair known as lanugo that covers the baby's skin inside the womb to fall off into the amniotic fluid. The baby will continue to drink the fluid (and everything else floating inside it) so the lanugo will ultimately form part of the baby's meconium.

**Day 212, Wednesday 8 March**

"Am I right in thinking boobs are the topic of our antenatal class tomorrow?" I asked Sarah as we unloaded the dishwasher.

"I think it's actually breastfeeding, but yes. Why?"

"I should probably know this, but I want to clarify something before we go. Just in case I embarrass myself."

"Ok..."

"How will the milk come out of your nipples? I imagine they're like shower heads, with milk being released from lots of openings?"

Sarah burst into laughter. "I don't think it's like that. They'll be like a cow's teat, with one hole in each nipple."

To find out the answer, I went looking for the copy of *Mothers and Others* we'd been given at the start of October. For once, I was right. Each nipple has between four and 20 holes. Even my own.


**Day 213, Thursday 9 March**

My time as a self-professed boob guru didn't last long. I never knew there were so many incorrect ways to breast-feed. For a start, I didn't expect quite so much breast to go into the baby's mouth. But as our instructor said, it's called breastfeeding, not nipple feeding.

I was impressed by the variety of colours breast milk can be. The initial production of colostrum is yellow and although the milk moves closer in appearance to cow's milk within a couple of weeks, some mothers produce milk that's white with a green or blue hue. We were assured it's nothing to worry about, so I might experiment by buying Sarah some Smarties.


**Day 214, Friday 10 March**

Our baby can see! We discovered this when we shone a light at Sarah's bump, which caused them to visibly move in the womb.

**Day 215, Saturday 11 March**

After drinking six pints at the antenatal class social, I've talked myself into leading a 'Dads and Babies' trip to watch Cambridge United's first home game next season.

Back at home, we watched the baby move underneath the two thick jumpers Sarah was wearing. I hope the promise of watching the U's always excites them this much.


**Day 216, Sunday 12 March**

Our antenatal course included a free online hypnobirthing programme. The name 'hypnobirthing' makes it sound like mumbo jumbo and to a natural cynic such as myself, it's like a red rag to a bull. Certainly, it's easy to dismiss when you learn one of the key tenets is the emphasis placed on language. Advocates maintain that by changing the words we use, the pain of labour - sorry birthing - can be reduced. The word 'pain' has negative connotations so it is itself replaced by the word 'power', while the terms 'surge' and 'blossoming' are used instead of 'contraction' and 'dilation'.

A 2015 study into hypnobirthing in the NHS found it made no difference to the method of birth or use of drugs to control pain. However, science has proved religious faith can relieve pain, so why can't positivity and breathing techniques?

After dinner we completed the first few modules. These emphasised that when 'birthing' Sarah should avoid spikes of adrenaline and focus on feeling relaxed to encourage the release of the hormone oxytocin, which will contract the uterus and progress the birth.

Which is all well and good in theory.

*Week 31*

## Day 218, Tuesday 14 March

This morning I told my boss of my intention to take four weeks off after the birth. The need to have such a conversation was so novel, I mistakenly told him I would be taking maternity, rather than paternity, leave. No wonder he looked confused.

## Day 219, Wednesday 15 March

Many people are still surprised - some even admit to being underwhelmed - by the size of Sarah's bump, but today at the midwife appointment it was measured as being exactly the size it should be: 31cm at 31 weeks. The baby is now the size of a coconut and their brain is developing at a faster rate than ever.

## Day 220, Thursday 16 March

We attended the final antenatal class this evening, which focused on first aid for babies. Perhaps this information is kept to last as it's the most important to remember, but it was a sombre subject on which to end.

I recalled some of the training from my time as a lifeguard, but there was plenty of information I'd long since forgotten, such as the fact you can use a defibrillator on a newborn. On a less distressing topic, I also learned that, as babies can't blow their own nose, plastic squeezy ice cream cone-shaped objects called 'nose suckers' can be used to unblock their nostrils. A task I'm sure neither I nor the baby will relish.

## Day 221, Friday 17 March

We left home for a final pre-baby weekend away together in soggy Suffolk. On the way we used our life family membership of the National Trust to visit Ickworth House.

"You know, I haven't seen more than two magpies the whole time since I've been pregnant," Sarah said as we walked around the grounds.

"I'm sorry?"

"You know, like the rhyme. One for sorrow, two for joy, three for a girl, four for a boy."

"Ah yes."

"This is the one time it's likely to be relevant, but I haven't seen three or four together."

There are times when I'm aware I've fallen short in my responsibilities as a father-to-be. I hadn't realised monitoring the local fowl was one of them.

While buying food for the weekend I redeemed myself by picking up a big box of dates. Many foods are believed to assist labour, but dates are among the very few to have been proven to do so.

Researchers at Jordan University of Science and Technology studied the effect of the fruit by analysing the labour of expectant mothers who had been eating six dates per day during the four weeks prior to their due date, compared to those who hadn't consumed any. The study found the women who had been eating the dates were 74% more dilated when they were admitted to give birth than the non-date eaters and that the first stage of labour lasted for 'only' 8.5 hours for them compared to 15 hours for those who did not consume any dates. So it's no surprise Sarah's friends have all been eating dates.

I was reluctant for Sarah to start too early for fear the food's superpowers might result in an early arrival, but the promise of an easier labour has proved impossible for Sarah to resist.

## Day 223, Mother's Day, Sunday 19 March

"This time next year, you'll get breakfast in bed," Sarah's mum told her over the phone.

It seems a bit harsh to expect the baby to be up to speed that quickly. Particularly as I'm not. I forgot it was Mother's Day and wholly overlooked the fact Sarah might have appreciated some chocolate in acknowledgement of her endeavours so far.

"It's not fair that I won't get a Mother's Day, but you'll get a Father's Day this year," she said in mock bitterness.

Turns out there are some benefits to not having an autumn baby after all.

*Week 32*

## Day 224, Monday 20 March

It's scary to think that, assuming Sarah's bump grows 1cm every week, she still has another 8cm to go. Developmentally this does make sense though, as over the next eight weeks the baby will gain approximately 40% of its total birth weight.

Tonight we received the news the first baby on our antenatal course has been born. We may have nearly two months to go until our own due date, but seeing the photos of their newborn daughter felt like we had collectively taken another step forward.

## Day 225, Tuesday 21 March

The birth of our fellow classmates' baby provided the impetus we needed to buy some of the items on Sarah's carefully curated pregnancy list.

We picked up a few essentials like water wipes and a thermometer and collected a free bag of baby products handed out to expectant mothers at the till. This contained nappies for newborns, Sudocrem and antibacterial gel.

I suspect it won't take long for our child to learn their parents love a freebie.

## Day 226, Wednesday 22 March

In an attempt to mitigate against the fact our study will soon be repurposed as a nursery, we've paid for a combined office and shed to be built at the end of our garden. Today, the ground screws went in. The weather has been miserable for weeks, but as long as it improves, the office should be here before the baby.

Sarah had been keen to requisition some of the office space for a chest freezer. A couple of years earlier, her mum had prepared for the arrival of her first grandchild by kindly preparing 200 frozen homemade meals for her daughter and son-in-law. The only problem was that when Sarah's sister suddenly needed to stop eating dairy products, it was left to her husband alone to work through six months' worth of lasagne.

Still, it seemed a good problem to have and Sarah's mum had offered to cook the same amount of food for us. We hoped that by telling Lola of Sarah's mum's generosity, we would spark her competitive spirit and we might receive enough food to last until Christmas. But alas. Rather than engaging in a game of one-upmanship, she pointed out various drawbacks to installing a chest freezer.

We eventually decided against getting one. If we had 10 children on our National Trust membership cards, such a purchase might be necessary. Until then, the one in the kitchen will suffice.

## Day 227, Thursday 23 March

I met up with the 'dads' from our antenatal class for another social. Ostensibly this was to watch England play Italy in a European Championship qualifier, but we spent most of the evening discussing baby-related topics. It's safe to say that if you'd told me in 2015 - the year before I met Sarah - that I'd be discussing collecting colostrum when Harry Kane became England's highest ever goalscorer, I wouldn't have believed you.

The father of the first baby to arrive even managed to join us for a drink. He received a hero's welcome.

## Day 228, Friday 24 March

Feeling the effects of the night before, I needed to stop twice to throw up while on a run with a friend this morning. It was another reminder that I'm not 25 any more.

## Day 229, Saturday 25 March

We resumed the hypnobirthing course after dinner and practised various breathing techniques. Unfortunately, any benefits we might have gained from the slow inhalation and exhalation of breath were undermined by our inability to stop yawning.

**Day 230, Sunday 26 March**

The hypnobirthing course came with a script to encourage the release of oxytocin into Sarah's bloodstream. I read it out numerous times, each time varying my intonation.

"...take a couple of moments now to breathe in the air around you and bask in the warmth and light of your self-belief."

I turned to look at Sarah, who was sitting with her eyes closed. "Do you think you'll find this useful?"

"No. Do you?"

"Not at all. If I was having contractions and they are anything like how I imagine, I wouldn't find it the least bit helpful. To be honest, I'd tell you to get lost."

Sarah smiled. "I might still get you to do it. If I'm in pain, you should suffer too."

*Week 33*

**Day 231, Monday 27 March**

Sarah is gaining around 500g of weight per week. Half of this goes straight onto the baby, which is now the size of a butternut squash. Sarah's belly is round and reassuringly firm, and looks as if she has swallowed a desktop globe.

**Day 232, Tuesday 28 March**

In the latest hypnobirthing video I was encouraged to mirror Sarah's breathing while staring intently into her eyes. The baby's growth over the past week has made Sarah breathless once again and she has returned to taking the deep, laboured breaths that marked the early weeks of the pregnancy. Mirroring this was hard work.

Mimicking Sarah's snoring was much more fun. She currently sounds like a warthog preparing for battle.

## Day 233, Wednesday 29 March

Tonight's hypnobirthing module taught me how to perform light touch massages to support Sarah when she was 'surging'. It also recommended the use of 'affirmation bunting'. This would involve sticking Post-it notes around the house to remind Sarah how well she was doing. It was suggested we could then take these down and bring them with us to the hospital.

Considering we still haven't hung any pictures on the walls, the chances of us putting up any bunting in the coming days is slim. And the chances of me having the presence of mind to take it all down when Sarah goes into labour is, frankly, zilch.

We listened to some affirmations narrated by the hypnobirthing instructor. I was pleased to discover Sarah found the instructor's voice as uninspiring as my own. The instructor encouraged us to listen to the affirmations passively to let them absorb into our subconscious. Before I zoned out entirely, I picked up a few of the words of wisdom. These included:

- I am a strong woman and a loving mother
- I travel the birthing pathway with an open mind
- My surges are the perfect strength for my birthing

I think I might skip reminding Sarah of the last one.

**Day 235, Friday 31 March**

After eating more than 70 dates over the past two weeks, the novelty has definitely worn off. Sarah never wants to see another date again.

One of the reasons the consumption of dates has become popular is because by softening the cervix they may reduce the risk of perineal tears. These are tears that occur between the vagina and the anus during childbirth. Around 90% of first-time mums who have a vaginal birth will have a tear, graze or episiotomy (a cut made by a doctor or midwife.)

Daily perineal massages in the weeks running up to the birth are recommended to minimise the possibility of tearing. Partners are encouraged to assist, but we haven't tried it yet. I've heard it's not very sexy, so I'll keep pushing the dates.

**Day 236, Saturday 1 April**

We watched the famously steamy film *Love & Other Drugs* before going to bed. I lay there holding Sarah, thinking about how our sex life had inevitably been affected by the pregnancy.

Admittedly, being able to feel the baby move when I slip my arm underneath the curve of her bump is extraordinary compensation.

*Week 34*

### Day 238, Monday 3 April

Sarah invited a few couples from our antenatal class to form a team for our local pub quiz. We managed to avoid coming last which, given the cerebral nature of many of our fellow competitors in Cambridge, we counted as a win.

As newcomers with three heavily pregnant women in tow, we were a conspicuous group and all three women were called upon to stand in the middle of the pub and pick the winning numbers of the charity raffle. Looking at Sarah's tummy button poke through her top, it was evident that she has indisputably 'popped'.

### Day 239, Tuesday 4 April

We're less than six weeks from the due date and my emotions are beginning to fluctuate wildly. One moment I'm full of eager anticipation, the next I'm preoccupied by unfounded worries about the baby's health.

### Day 240, Wednesday 5 April

Sarah is fed up with buying baby-related products. The list of mattress protectors, socks and babygrows we need seems endless.

One of the less mundane - but eye-wateringly expensive - items we would like is a cargo bike. These bicycles are a common sight in Cambridge and have a cart at the front which can carry children (and/or shopping).

Taking one for a test ride at this stage might seem as unnecessarily pre-emptive as scouting out nurseries when you're only a few months pregnant, but the lead time to have them sent from - you guessed it - the Netherlands, is long. Babies can travel in a car seat in the cart when they are three months old so hopefully the bike would help to alleviate the sense of cabin fever brought about by caring for a newborn.

We were heading home from a test ride when Sarah told me of a less enjoyable task.

"We need to wash all the clothes and sheets for the baby."

I groaned, thinking of the mountains of clothes that filled our loft. "Is that really necessary? The secondhand stuff has been washed and the new stuff is, well, new."

"According to where I was looking online, it is. The baby's skin shouldn't come into contact with irritants."

"Where did you read this? Hypochondria.com?"

"No. And it wasn't on Persil.com either."

Our washing machine is going to be put through its paces earlier than I'd anticipated.


## Day 241, Thursday 6 April

Sarah returned from a routine appointment with the midwife with mixed news. The good news is that Sarah's test results look healthy and the baby seems to have moved into a head-first position. Sarah had guessed as much, having recently felt kicks near her diaphragm.

On a less positive note, Sarah was measured as small for her gestational age. At 34 weeks Sarah's bump (technically known as her fundal height) should be 34cm, but now it's apparently only 29cm. Given that it was recorded as being 31cm three weeks ago, and is considerably larger now, it seems like somewhere along the line someone made a mistake with the measuring tape.

The midwife booked Sarah into the next possible

appointment with a sonographer. These were in short supply the afternoon before the Easter Bank Holiday weekend, but we were seen that evening.

I marvelled once again at the details picked up by the ultrasound. We could see the atrium and ventricles of the baby's heart and watch as hiccups caused their torso to spasmodically contract. To avoid finding out the baby's gender, we were told to look away when the sonographer moved the transducer towards the baby's groin. We hadn't been instructed to do so at the 28-week scan (which I had taken to indicate we're having a girl), so the sonographer's comment today has put the cat among the pigeons.

After recording all of the measurements, the sonographer was able to reassure us the baby looked well. Remarkably, although Sarah's bump is smaller than would be expected, the baby, at 5lb 8oz (2.5kg), is actually larger than average. They must be pretty cramped in there. The baby has continued to grow at the same rate as before which is good, but this means they still have short legs and a very fat stomach. Indeed, our baby's abdominal circumference is nearly equal to that of their head.

### Day 242, Good Friday 7 April

Upon arriving at my parents' house for the Easter weekend, Mum handed us a baby doll to carry around. The idea is this will help their dog, Jack, adapt more quickly to not being number one when the baby arrives and he'll understand the need to be gentle when near them. We were instructed to sleep next to the doll too so that it becomes infused with our pheromones, as this will supposedly convince Jack the practice doll is human.

**Day 243, Saturday 8 April**

Sleeping next to the doll felt odd. Mainly because I'm not a five-year-old girl, but also because of the warnings we'd heard about how important it is *not* to share your bed with your baby due to the risk of suffocation.

I thought Jack would have little interest in the doll, but I couldn't have been more wrong. Whenever I hold it in my arms he points his nose towards it and his ears stand up on end. However, I'm not convinced his curiosity extends beyond an eagerness to find out whether the doll is a new plastic toy for him to destroy.

*Week 35*

**Day 245, Monday 10 April**

I turned 34 today. It felt strange as I remember my parents being in their mid-thirties. Our child won't be able to say that.

**Day 247, Wednesday 12 April**

Sarah's difficulty breathing is causing her to appear irritated by everything.

"Are you ok?" I asked, trying to ascertain if I'd done something wrong.

"I'm fine."

"You seem disgruntled."

"Well, I'm not."

"Ok," I said. "It's just you *sound* quite passive aggressive."

"So would you if your internal organs were being

squashed by the growth of a giant baby that won't stop kicking you."

I placed my hands on Sarah's stomach and felt the baby kick unhelpfully at the end of each deep exhale, as if they were scared the walls around them would close in entirely.

"Point taken."

## Day 248, Thursday 13 April

This evening I held Sarah close as we lay in bed facing each other under the duvet. To my astonishment I could feel the baby's kicks against my crotch. It was one of the most peculiar sensations I've ever experienced.

## Day 249, Friday 14 April

Unsure of how many opportunities we'll have to do so in the near future, Sarah and I went out for dinner.

Reflecting on her pregnancy so far, Sarah admitted she's found it tougher than expected and everyday activities, such as putting on trainers, have now become difficult. Considering Sarah looks like she's carrying a bowling ball under her jumper, this is hardly surprising.

During pregnancy women gain about 26.5lb (12kg). The baby accounts for approximately 7.7lb (3.5kg) of this, with the remainder made up of:

6.6lb (3kg) of fat
4.4lb (2kg) of fluid and blood
2.2lb (1kg) of additional weight on each breast
2.2lb (1kg) of additional uterine weight
2.2lb (1kg) of amniotic fluid
1.5lb (0.7kg) of placenta

I'm amazed people choose to put themselves through pregnancy five, six or seven times. If nothing else, it's a long time to spend not feeling your best. I can't help but come to the conclusion, as others have before me, that if it were men who became pregnant, the global population would be significantly smaller.

## Day 250, Saturday 15 April

We've ticked off another under-celebrated pregnancy milestone. In our case, 250 days coincided with a genuine landmark though as today marked one month until the due date.

## Day 251, Sunday 16 April

A weekend doesn't seem to go by without us picking up secondhand stuff for the baby. Today we collected a changing table for £20.

The child for whom it was originally bought watched on in dismay as we wedged the changing table into our car. The time has come for it to be decorated in another baby's urine.

*Week 36*

## Day 252, Monday 17 April

The baby's lungs are now fully formed and ready to take their first breath when they are born. They are also slowly shedding the vernix caseosa that covers and protects their skin.

## Day 253, Tuesday 18 April

Sarah's bump continues to vary in unexpected ways. Sometimes it feels like a reassuringly robust protective shell. At others, it feels soft as if the baby has retreated into a previously undiscovered corner of the womb. And occasionally it's hard like a bag of marbles, with indistinguishable limbs poking out in all directions.

The latter may be Braxton Hicks contractions. Some women never feel these tightenings of the uterus, but to others they feel like the onset of labour. Either way, they're nothing to worry about and, as far as we can tell, the timing of each tightening is arbitrary.

## Day 254, Wednesday 19 April

This afternoon we had our 36-week scan, the second of our two additional scans we have as part of the research programme. Sarah cycled directly from work, while I drove to familiarise myself with the route from our house to the hospital.

If our modes of transport seem counterintuitive, so too is the fact the baby gets more difficult to see on the ultrasound scan the larger it gets. This is because the tangle of limbs makes it tricky to distinguish a knee from an elbow.

The sonographer struggled to obtain the measurements she needed from our fidgety foetus. Sarah, lying on her back, soon began to feel faint. The weight of the baby was constricting her blood flow and it was only after drinking water and lying on her side for a few minutes that she felt better.

Tonight Sarah had a pregnancy massage from a prenatal therapist. This was a present bought by her friends, who correctly guessed I hadn't thought to organise something similar myself.

I stayed downstairs while Sarah had her sides, stomach and legs massaged to the backdrop of whale noises. When I came upstairs a few hours later, the smell of scented candles and massage oil still filled our bedroom.

## Day 255, Thursday 20 April

We returned to the hospital for a midwife appointment and a tour of the birth centre. Each of the 10 spacious private rooms contained a birthing pool (which looked like a six-person hot tub) for water births, a double bed, an ensuite shower and a toilet. It's a wonderful facility often talked about in hallowed terms, but one that relatively few women end up utilising due to the complexities of labour. Most give birth on the delivery unit instead.

The midwife was full of advice and encouraged Sarah to start harvesting colostrum next week. "It's good to get used to manhandling your breasts. Normally we never think about it and leave our partners to do the manhandling," she said looking pointedly in my direction, "but you have so many skills you'll need to acquire in the weeks ahead, it's good to get this one down while you can."

Sarah's bump measured small once again. She was asked to visit the sonography department, but I needed to go back to work so I reluctantly left her at the hospital. After our previous experience, we agreed the scan would most likely confirm Sarah was just carrying small.

It turned out not to be quite so straightforward. The sonographer was concerned the baby's stomach had shrunk. She referred Sarah to a consultant, who put the anomaly down to an incorrect measurement at the previous scan and sent Sarah home.

## Day 256, Friday 21 April

This evening Kat and Sean arrived with Max. I'm astounded by how much he's grown already. No longer a newborn baby, his personality is rapidly developing and he frequently flashes his cheeky smile. Seeing him has intensified my excitement at having a child of our own.


## Day 258, Sunday 23 April

As we go to bed Sarah briefly chokes on some of the excess saliva she's producing as a result of the pregnancy. Who said the third trimester wasn't sexy?


*Week 37*


## Day 259, Monday 24 April

Until today I believed I would always find Sarah's boobs titillating. But that was before we tried harvesting colostrum.

I didn't have a clue what it was when one of the mothers-to-be asked a question about it in our first antenatal class. Without delving too deeply into the subject, I decided it sounded like a niche custom performed by members of cults.

The official NHS guidance states the practice is unnecessary if you're having a healthy pregnancy. Colostrum is the first form of milk and is packed full of antibodies and immunoglobulins (whatever they are). It provides the baby with an early boost to their immune system and for this reason is sometimes described as a baby's first vaccination.

Hopefully, our baby will latch seamlessly when Sarah begins breastfeeding and any colostrum collected prior to their arrival therefore won't be needed. Nonetheless, we were advised that it may come in handy if the baby doesn't latch easily, as babies can consume crucial calories by sucking a finger dipped in colostrum. Some people think harvesting colostrum during pregnancy may also increase its production immediately after the birth.

So Sarah wanted to give it a go. I envisioned a scene charged with eroticism, but I couldn't have been more wrong. As she stepped out of the shower Sarah began to massage and squeeze her boobs in a perfunctory manner while I stood there with a syringe in my hand.

Beads of colostrum began to appear from Sarah's nipple like sap from a tree. This caught us both off guard. If we hadn't already had the discussion about whether nipples were like shower heads, Sarah would have been worried. As it was, she kept squeezing the colostrum out until her nipple weeped like a kneecap scarred by carpet burn.

I was seeing Sarah's boobs - indeed all boobs - in a whole new light. These were not, I realised, boobs at all. They were breasts. It was like finding out jumpers could be used for something other than goal posts.

I found it distressing to watch the effect the process was having on this object of my desire. Sarah didn't experience any pain though. In fact, I recognised the zealous determination some people - ok, I - have when squeezing a particularly pernicious spot.

"Please can we stop?" I asked.

"Not yet," Sarah replied, not taking her eyes off her breast. "I just want to try a few more angles."

I stood there for several more minutes, my eyes fixed on her nipple to ensure I collected every drop of colostrum that emerged. I too was naked, ready for my own shower, and in the silence, I marvelled at how this deeply intimate act felt so platonic. Observing this scene would have caused my teenage brain to explode. *What? How? Why? Am I gay?*

"That's enough," I said, bringing myself back to the present and focusing my attention on the 0.1ml of translucent, muddy yellow liquid in the syringe.

"Fine. We'll start on the other one and we'll go back to this one."

Eventually, after collecting 0.3ml, Sarah allowed us to call it a night. But before I could jump in the shower, I was dispatched downstairs to put the fruits of our labour in the freezer. Going through the cold, dark house, I was pleased we'd decided against putting a chest freezer at the end of the garden.

## Day 260, Tuesday 25 April

The last eight and a half months have been filled with revelations. One of the most welcome has been the discovery of medjool dates. I'd never eaten them before, but now they are a part of Sarah's daily routine, I've grown rather partial to them. I certainly like them more than she does.

This week the pregnancy is considered to have reached full-term. Sarah is eager for the baby to arrive, but I still have a long list of chores to complete before the birth, so while we continue to bulk buy dates, I'm reluctant for Sarah to start cooking spicy curries quite yet.

## Day 261, Wednesday 26 April

Over breakfast I showed Sarah a study indicating that people with surnames near the start of the alphabet gain benefits those further down do not. It's another reason I'm pleased our child will be an Atkin.

We thought about not following the patriarchal tradition of using my last name and briefly considered adopting the modern trend of contracting our two surnames to create an entirely new surname for our child. But we couldn't come up with an alternative that avoided making our children sound like they were villainous characters in a Roald Dahl book.

## Day 262, Thursday 27 April

Sarah is determined to do all she can to ensure the baby arrives punctually and is spending more time than ever on her birthing ball. It's a slightly larger version of a Swiss ball. The ball is designed to reduce back pain and bouncing on it is believed to encourage the baby to move into the correct position.

Chatting to Sarah when she's bouncing on the ball feels like an interaction with an over-excited child. Which at least makes a change from her passive aggressive-sounding heavy breathing.

## Day 263, Friday 28 April

I travelled to Bristol for Peter's stag do. In the run-up I'd bristled when one of my friends suggested the weekend was to be my swansong, but it's true I won't have another weekend like it for some time.

I spent part of this evening playing beer bong with strippers who set me the challenge of bouncing the ball off one of their buttocks and off the cleavage of another before landing it in a cup.

I failed. What can I say? I was distracted.

I was punished for my shortcomings by being whipped by a leather belt. Perhaps it's no bad thing if this weekend does prove to be the swansong to my child-free existence.

## Day 265, Sunday 30 April

Mum drove me home at the end of the stag do, having stayed on the outskirts of Bristol over the weekend in case Sarah went into labour. She's a star. Playing a hybrid version of crazy golf and beer pong with strippers while tipsy was surreal. Doing it stone cold sober would have been plain weird.

Sarah's parents spent the weekend in Cambridge in case Sarah needed to go to hospital. As she didn't, Sarah's mum thoughtfully cooked and decanted 10 boxes of chicken pie and vegetarian chilli into our freezer. Not six months' worth to be sure, but enough to fill several drawers.

When everyone had departed, Sarah sat on my lap as we discussed our contrasting weekends. I could tell Sarah's getting bigger by the discomfort I felt in my squashed thighs.

*Week 38*

## Day 266, Early May Bank Holiday, Monday 1 May

We spent the first May Bank Holiday completing chores in readiness for the birth. After the debauchery of the weekend, I've come back to Earth with a bump.

## Day 267, Tuesday 2 May

Upon returning from work, Sarah told me she knocked into a man in the office canteen. She misjudged her current size and instead of sliding smoothly past him, her belly collided with his mug of hot tea. The poor man was mortified.

**Day 268, Wednesday 3 May**

Another late night colostrum harvesting session. It still feels bizarre.

**Day 269, Thursday 4 May**

Local elections have been held across the country. When I asked Sarah this morning if she intended to vote, she admitted she'd forgotten to register.

"But I reminded you..."

"I know, but I was busy carrying your child." This is a retort Sarah is turning to with increasing regularity.

"Think of your civic duty," I said in gentle admonishment.

"I am - I'm nurturing the next generation."

I gave up, knowing I had no comeback to this. The pregnancy is Sarah's immutable trump card.

Instead of going to the polls, Sarah went to another midwife appointment. The midwife took some cursory measurements of Sarah's bump and declared it to be a normal size. Hooray!

**Day 271, Coronation Day, Saturday 6 May**

I tend to let royal events pass me by - I remember watching Prince William's wedding in the fugue of a horrendous hangover on one of my last days at university - but Sarah was keen to get out of the house. So we went to Ely Cathedral, where they were showing the coverage of King Charles III's coronation and handing out free Pimms.

We could see the baby moving through Sarah's clothes during the pomp and ceremony of the service. They were particularly active during the performance of Welsh opera song *Kyrie Eleison*. Whether this was in delight or confusion at the Welsh language wasn't clear.

When we returned home I tried out the Transcutaneous Electrical Nerve Stimulation (TENS) machine we've borrowed from a friend. This small, battery-powered device is commonly used during the early stages of labour. It emits electrical pulses which are believed to reduce pain signals going to the brain and may stimulate the production of endorphins.

While I will never be able to appreciate the powerful sensation of a contraction, I wanted to understand what these electrical pulses felt like.

The worst part happened before we'd even turned on the machine. Sarah put the cold, sticky pads on my bare back before I was ready, causing me to squeal and arch my spine. I received no sympathy.

We started ramping up the frequency and intensity of the pulses to see whether I could handle it. I don't know about Sarah, but I gained a perverse and unexpected pleasure from this experiment. I like to think it was simple curiosity, yet maybe being whipped at the stag do had unlocked something in me. My skin tingled, but the pulses weren't painful.

By the time we reached the machine's limit, I must have looked like Frankenstein's monster, for I writhed as the high frequency electrical current flowed into me.


**Day 272, Sunday 7 May**

The King's coronation may have dominated the headlines, but there was another, more important event this weekend for members of the Yellow and Black Army. It was the final match of the season and to avoid relegation Cambridge

United needed to win and hope two other teams failed to do so.

Cambridge did their bit and when word filtered through to the stands that the others had not, my friends and I joined the fans pouring onto the pitch. The players were hoisted onto supporters' shoulders and yellow smoke flares were waved in the warm sunshine.

And to think I nearly didn't go in case Sarah went into labour.

Peter attended the match along with some dads from our antenatal class. When the dads returned to childcare duties, Peter and I went for a celebratory drink with Sarah. Sipping beers while overlooking the Cam, it was disconcerting to think we'll soon have a baby. We'd always assumed by this point that even if we didn't feel ready to become parents, we would at least be able to imagine caring for a newborn. Yet we still can't.

## Week 39

### Day 273, Coronation Bank Holiday, Monday 8 May

We used what remained of the long weekend to move items from the study into the newly finished garden office. As I feathered the nest of my new man cave, Sarah set about preparing the nursery. By the time we put the cot, chest of drawers and changing table in there, there wasn't enough space to swing a cat.

All three pieces of furniture are discordant shades of cheap wood, but considering they cost a combined total of £20, they'll do just fine. The saving grace is the sticker display Sarah has put on the wall, which depicts a rural scene populated by monkeys, zebras and elephants.

**Day 274, Tuesday 9 May**

Asked to pick up some nappy bags, this morning I made my first visit to the baby aisle in Tesco. I haven't felt so bewildered and as much of a fraud since I bought condoms for the first time. Unlike the condoms, hopefully I won't have to wait three years to use the nappy bags.

**Day 275, Wednesday 10 May**

We filled in our NHS birth plan together this evening. The first question concerned where Sarah wanted to give birth. Neither of us want the baby to be delivered at home and we're still hoping Sarah will be able to use the birth centre. Remaining in the comfort of your own living room is a nice idea, but for something so important, we want to be near plenty of medical experts. Around 45% of first-time mums who intend to stay at home end up in hospital during or just after the birth anyway.

Another of the questions required Sarah to predict the positions she would adopt during labour. Given her lack of experience, this was tricky to answer.

**Day 276, Thursday 11 May**

Sarah woke with yellow hands. Alarmed, she looked online for possible causes and wasn't surprised to find that, like practically everything, it could be a symptom of a pregnancy complication.

We were due at the hospital anyway at 8am for Sarah's next ultrasound appointment. Cycling behind Sarah on the way there, I noticed how the slit up the back of her shirt revealed the top of her maternity trousers. To the unknowing eye, the additional black material around her waist and lower back looked like huge incontinence pants or some sort of lumbar support. Few people who saw it would have guessed they had been overtaken by a woman just shy of 40 weeks pregnant. Even fewer would want to admit it.

Happily, the baby seems to be doing well. The sonographer reassured us about the size of the baby's stomach and pointed out the hair floating in the amniotic fluid around their head. The sonographer was also able to tell us the baby's legs had grown significantly. They're now longer than average. Just like ours.

The baby is estimated to weigh 7lb 8oz (3.4kg), a fraction more than the average birth weight of a baby. It goes to show, foetuses grow at different rates. Comparing each to the statistical average on any particular day may produce eye-catching results, but in most cases growth spurts balance out over time.

At the end of the appointment we asked the sonographer if she knew what might have caused Sarah's hands to turn yellow. As was only to be expected, she didn't know. We connected the dots ourselves while waiting in the reception area - Sarah had spent the previous evening shelling pomegranates.

**Day 277, Friday 12 May**

Sarah returned from her final day of work before maternity leave in an unsettled, restless mood. She won't be returning to the office for at least seven months and now feels trapped in limbo, not knowing what to do with herself until the baby arrives and without any idea of how long the wait may be.

**Day 278, Saturday 13 May**

Not to be outdone by my attendance of Peter's stag do, Sarah had intended to go to a hen do in London this afternoon. An hour before she was due to leave, her mum talked her out of it, reminding her - not unreasonably given Sarah is now just two days from her due date - that giving birth on the train wouldn't be much fun.

*Week 40*

**Day 280, Monday 15 May**

Our due date has come and gone. We're far from unique in this regard as nearly half of babies are born after their due date and only 5% of women give birth on the predicted day. If we were in France, we wouldn't even be overdue yet as pregnancy is expected to last 41 weeks.

Pregnant women can receive a membrane sweep at 40 weeks, and it's an indication of Sarah's desire for the baby to arrive that she had it on the first day she could. During a sweep a midwife puts a finger into the expectant mother's cervix and waggles it around in an attempt to stimulate the body to go into labour in the hours that follow. To Sarah's disappointment, her body wasn't quite ready, so the sweep of her cervix was more of a tickle.

The midwife was able to tell Sarah she's three fifths engaged though, meaning the baby's head is slowly dropping into her pelvis. She suggested lots of sex and nipple stimulation might bring the baby's arrival forward. I didn't even have to pay her!

**Day 281, Tuesday 16 May (1 day overdue)**

We're the only couple in our antenatal class yet to give birth. The mothers have been meeting weekly, but as Sarah's only just begun her maternity leave, today was the first occasion she could join them. Unfortunately after catching up with everyone, she experienced pelvic pain walking home and by this evening could only shuffle across the living room.

One in five pregnant women struggle with pelvic pain at some point. While she was putting her feet up, Sarah researched more ways to induce spontaneous labour. There's disappointingly little evidence that sex helps. However, semen is rich in prostaglandin, which is present when the cervix softens in early labour and is the compound used during hospital inductions. Sexual activity also boosts the production of oxytocin. Both of which are good enough reasons for me.

There's more evidence regarding the benefits of nipple stimulation. Yet I was taken aback by the necessary time commitment. Studies show the practice increased the number of women who went into labour within 72 hours - if their breasts were massaged "for a total of one to three hours a day". *Three hours?!* I'm trying to earn a crust. My colleagues will understand if I cancel meetings when Sarah needs to go to hospital to give birth, but they'd quite rightly have something to say if I cancelled meetings because I had cramp from fondling my wife's breasts.

Sarah cooked a hot curry for dinner in the hope it might move things along. It hasn't seemed to have had any immediate effect, other than to make my nose run. Which doubtless made the prospect of making love all the more appealing.

## Day 282, Wednesday 17 May (2 days overdue)

Since the start of the week, Sarah's emotions have become noticeably more intense and she oscillates between tetchiness and tears as feelings of frustration, pain and anxiety coalesce. So far, we've received several messages from our mums. Both had agreed they didn't need to be notified immediately if Sarah went into labour, but have nevertheless sent messages every day asking for updates.

As per the guidance, Sarah had packed a bag containing what we might need at the hospital. It was about time I had a look inside. A midwife had recommended that I repacked it myself as otherwise, when push comes to shove, I wouldn't be able to find everything Sarah had squirrelled away. After piling snacks, maternity pads, Sarah's pyjamas and a variety of other items on the living room floor, I put them all back in the bag, along with some underwear for me in case we end up staying at the hospital longer than we hope.

## Day 283, Thursday 18 May (3 days overdue)

Sarah remains lethargic and sore. She's felt much worse since starting maternity leave, which may be because her body finally has a chance to rest and recover in preparation for what lies ahead.

Meanwhile I've bought a secondhand cargo bike. I cycled it 15 miles home this morning, familiarising myself with our new mode of transport as I passed through villages of wisteria-covered thatched houses in south Cambridgeshire.

The bike and Sarah's current physical condition bear certain similarities. Both are heavy, slow and have wide turning circles, yet retain an inherent degree of charm and aesthetic appeal.

The bike has already accumulated thousands of miles in the Netherlands, but it is by far the most expensive bike either of us have ever owned. Many couples would have spent the £1,500 it cost on a shiny new pram, but hopefully we'll still be using the bike in 10 years' time - long after we've sold our pram.

## Day 284, Friday 19 May (4 days overdue)

I was sure today would be the day. While out running in drizzly rain with a friend, he told me his wife had been due to give birth on a Monday and did so the following Friday. Then, as I returned home, I saw a nesting swan I often passed on the riverbank now had her mate by her side and a tiny cygnet under her wing. I stopped to watch them.

A man, a bit younger than myself who I presumed was on his way to work at one of the nearby science parks, cycled past before looping back to see what I was looking at.

"It's an impressive nest isn't it?" he said.

"Yes. I've seen a swan here for months, but it's the first time I've seen the cygnet." When the cyclist didn't respond, I mused, "I wonder when the cygnet was born."

He remained silent. A minute later he suddenly exclaimed, "Look, they have a baby!"

"Yes," I smiled. I think I've found the next David Attenborough.

## Day 285, Saturday, 20 May (5 days overdue)

At 4.45pm Mum texted me. "Just over seven hours to have a Taurus. Do you think you can do it?"

I looked across the garden to Sarah who was happily reading a book. "It seems unlikely," I replied.

Mum has a theory that if the baby is born a Taurus they will be a boy, but if they're a Gemini, they will be a girl. I scoffed at this, but her logic is as reasonable as any I can offer in support of my conviction that we have a daughter on the way.

Within minutes, Mum sent me a list of reputed Gemini character traits, along with a link to an article in *Cosmopolitan* which cited Donald Trump, Kanye West and Angelina Jolie as prime examples of a Gemini. From this, Mum concluded that Gemini children "sound exhausting". I'm not too perturbed, as I don't pay much attention to the horoscope pages of magazines, but the article does suggest our child will be a "notorious gossip" which, if they're anything like me, probably will be the case.

### Day 286, Sunday, 21 May (6 days overdue)

Sarah never experienced the anticipated spike in her libido during the second trimester. But now she's been told sex might lead to labour, Sarah's as amorous as a left wing activist on election night. I'd take it as a compliment, but I'm not sure I've got much to do with it.

### *Week 41*

### Day 287, Monday 22 May (7 days overdue)

When I woke Sarah, she stretched her arms out with a look of disappointment on her face. She appreciates her sleep, so often does this, but in recent days Sarah has been more displeased than usual. She's read that due to the increased levels of melatonin produced at night, she is more likely to go into labour then. So every morning she awakes having not experienced contractions means she probably has at least another day to wait.

I gave her a kiss.

"You were better at getting this baby in me than you are getting it out of me," Sarah said with a wry smile.

After breakfast we attended a midwife appointment, anticipating they would want to talk about the options for inducing the pregnancy.

Medical science has progressed since the 1980s and it's now unlikely Mum would carry me to nearly 44 weeks. The chances of a stillbirth increase from less than one in 1,000 at 40 weeks to three in 1,000 after 41 weeks. For this reason, if, by week 41, a woman isn't showing signs of imminently going into labour, most doctors will advise her to receive assistance to initiate the process.

We discussed the possible paths ahead, all the while hoping they'd be made redundant by Sarah going into labour naturally within a few hours. It was agreed Sarah would have another membrane sweep today, with a third scheduled for two days' time. If this didn't have the desired effect, Sarah would go to the hospital on Friday to be induced. At this point she would have a prosthetic device called a pessary inserted. The pessary contains prostaglandin and usually causes labour to begin within 24 hours.

If that didn't do the trick, we'd then come back to the hospital for Sarah to be examined. If, by this point, her cervix had dilated a couple of centimetres, Sarah's waters would be artificially broken to encourage her womb to contract and bring on labour. If her cervix hadn't sufficiently dilated, Sarah would receive two more pessaries. If these didn't work, there would be a 24-hour pause to allow her body to recover from the sudden influx of hormones. Once this ended Sarah would be put on an intravenous drip of synthetic oxytocin.

Clearly, this is a lot to go through before you even begin going into labour.

Sarah's cervix remains resolutely shut so, once again, a full membrane sweep wasn't possible today.

I suspect we'll be back on Wednesday.


## Day 289, Wednesday 24 May (9 days overdue)

The midwife performing the membrane sweep sensed Sarah's wish to avoid being induced and vowed to do her best to encourage the onset of contractions. She was, by her own admission, "thorough". Sarah barely flinched, even as she began to bleed, and impressed the midwife with her capacity to tolerate pain.

"Labour won't be a problem for you," she said.

Sarah's cervix had changed little since Monday and the rest of the day has passed without incident.

The last of my school friends to have a birthday in May celebrated his today. If our baby was staying put to avoid sharing their name with one of my friends, they've managed it.


## Day 290, Thursday 25 May (10 days overdue)

Sarah measured small again yesterday, so she cycled to the hospital this morning for another scan. The sonographer recorded the baby's dimensions and happily announced that by her estimations, the baby would weigh 8lb 5 oz (3.8kg). Sarah was rather less enthused by the baby's growing size.

Last month I bought tickets to see a T20 cricket match at

Lord's as part of a stag do in London tonight. Given Sarah's rate of progress, it seems unlikely I'd miss much, but travelling to the capital when Sarah is so far overdue feels like I'm asking for trouble. Reluctantly, I decided not to go.

I drowned my sorrows at the Cambridge Beer Festival, where I met Sarah on her way back from hospital. It's tricky to drown sorrows when you're limited to just one pint, but I knew any brownie points I accrued for not travelling to London would quickly be forgotten if Sarah went into labour while I was over the legal limit to drive.

### Day 291, Friday 26 May (11 days overdue)

At 6am Sarah noticed the bedsheet was wet. Her waters had broken.

In case of such an event, Sarah had slept on top of a mattress protector since the due date. However, when we stripped the bedsheet we discovered the papery protector had scrunched up over the course of the week and migrated to my side of the bed. Where it wasn't much use.

We called the hospital and were asked to come in. The midwife examined Sarah and sent us back home with instructions to call again when Sarah began to feel regular, powerful contractions. If she didn't within 24 hours, she was told she would need to return to be induced as the chance of infection increases beyond this point.

The waiting game began.

According to the NHS, 60% of women go into labour within 24 hours of their waters breaking. We tried everything to kickstart contractions. We went for a walk, climbed stairs sideways, drank herbal tea and harvested colostrum. But to no avail. Now Sarah's waters had broken, sex was out of the question, so instead we tried to get Sarah's oxytocin levels flowing by watching 2004 romcom

*13 going on 30*. When that too didn't work, we gave up and went to bed.

## Day 292, Saturday 27 May (12 days overdue)

"Chris, wake up. I'm bleeding."

We'd only been asleep for a few hours, but with those words, I was wide awake.

When Sarah called the hospital the midwives explained it was most likely the remnant of her mucus plug, or 'show'. Normally this plug of mucus comes away from the cervix before the waters break, but it seemed to be the other way round for Sarah. Amniotic fluid continued to leak from her womb, making the blood look more copious than it was. We were told to keep monitoring the baby's movements and get some rest before attending the hospital in the morning.

At the maternity assessment unit, they measured the baby's movements and heart rate while we waited for a bed to become available. A couple of hours later we were led into a small room and abruptly told we wouldn't be leaving until we'd had the baby. The room was perfectly functional, but it was a far cry from those in the birth centre.

When Sarah received a six-hour pessary a little later, a midwife explained that due to the length of time since her waters had broken, it was better to have the baby on the delivery unit.

While the pessary took effect, I went in search of lunch. Addenbrooke's is the last NHS hospital to have a Burger King and it's only the prohibitive cost of buying out the fast-food restaurant's lease contract that has kept it in situ. Knowing neither Sarah nor the midwives would be impressed if I returned to the delivery unit with two Bacon Double Cheeseburgers, I discarded the evidence of my own lunch and bought Sarah a sandwich from M&S.

During the six-hour wait, we were permitted to wander outside in the sunshine. Sarah gradually felt her contractions become more regular, until they were occurring twice every 10 minutes. Women are encouraged to go to hospital when they're regularly having three contractions in this time frame, so Sarah was pleased by the low level of discomfort she was experiencing. Perhaps, she dared to suggest, her labour might not be quite as difficult as she'd imagined.

This optimism didn't last long.

The midwives were happy with her progress at the end of the six hours, but Sarah was struggling to cope with the increasing intensity of the contractions. She was on all fours on the bed and breathing hard. Neither the TENS machine nor the hypnobirthing techniques were proving effective distractions.

It was difficult watching Sarah suffer like this. Unable to think of anything helpful to say, I attempted to ease Sarah's pain by rubbing her lower back. She appreciated the gesture, but we both knew it made little difference. I was a parasol on a planet about to crash into the sun.

Sarah was prescribed paracetamol and dihydrocodeine tablets to relieve the pain. When this proved insufficient, she tried Entonox (a mixture of 50% nitrous oxide and 50% oxygen, also known as gas and air), but found it made her nauseous. Her reluctance to seek more extreme pain relief, such as an injection of pethidine or to have an epidural, remained unwavering.

At 10pm the midwives brought Sarah a microwavable chicken jalfrezi for dinner. Within an hour of forcing herself to eat it, she'd thrown it back up into a cardboard dish. I fetched another litre-capacity dish just before it overflowed, knowing we wouldn't be ordering a jalfrezi again any time in the near future.

**Day 293, Sunday 28 May (13 days overdue)**

Sarah continued to bring up large quantities of orange-coloured water, rice and, eventually, grey bile. By the time she ceased, it was light outside. The vomiting may have been caused by the dihydrocodeine, but it might simply have been her body's reaction to the pain of the contractions. Sarah needed to preserve every ounce of strength she had, and throwing up was visibly weakening her. She was put on an intravenous drip to keep her fluid levels up.

In between retches, Sarah was moved into a larger room in the delivery unit with a birth pool. In spite of my best efforts, I couldn't keep myself awake and I fell asleep in an armchair for 15 minutes. It's the only sleep either of us got.

*5am*

The midwife announced the baby would arrive within four hours. She hoped this prediction would spur Sarah on, but the idea of another four hours of contractions appalled her.

Sarah entered the birth pool to try something different and immediately felt the benefit of the water's buoyancy.

The novelty soon wore off though.

*7.30am*

Sarah carefully got out of the pool to allow the midwife to assess her progress. As she lay on the bed, I noticed grazes on her kneecaps. She'd been straining so hard, she hadn't even realised she'd hurt them in the pool.

*8am*

The midwife who had been with us overnight finished her shift and we were taken into the care of a new senior midwife and student. I was so tired I was struggling not to slide off the edge of the birth pool I was leaning against. I'd long since run out of words of encouragement for Sarah. When a contraction occurred, I just gently stroked her arm and repeated the same meaningless phrases. There are only so many ways you can say "you're doing really well".

No one said it, but it didn't take a degree in midwifery to see that while Sarah was doing her best, it wasn't enough. For want of a better description, she looked constipated and the baby - as much as I could tell from my intentionally restricted viewpoint - seemed unlikely to appear any time soon.

I'd been warned that watching the birth would be tough and had braced myself for the struggle of the final furlong. What I hadn't foreseen was the psychological challenge of observing the person I love endure such hardship for so many hours.

The instructor in the hypnobirthing video claimed giving birth could be a "really positive experience". Not from where I was standing. Blood and faeces continued to emerge, but it was Sarah's pained whimpering I found most difficult to bear. Anyone who considers the birth of their child as the greatest day of their lives must have a complete disregard for their partner's wellbeing. I knew that even when the baby arrived, it would be far from the best day of my life. It wasn't even the best day of the calendar month. Celebrating Cambridge's survival in League One on 7 May was infinitely more enjoyable.

## 10.20am

The baby's predicted 9am arrival time had sailed by when a doctor entered the room and told Sarah she intended to make sure the baby had arrived by 11am. This was to ensure the baby's journey through the birth canal didn't last longer than the recommended three hours. The doctor told Sarah that unless the baby arrived within 20 minutes, she would try to extract the baby using a ventouse (a suction cup) attached to the baby's head. If that didn't work, she'd use forceps.

The midwives remained confident Sarah could give birth without the instruments and urged her to redouble her efforts. Sarah didn't have anything extra to give, but began making progress by using her right leg to push hard against the midwife's shoulder. As she did, I could see sinews in her body tensing in places I didn't even know she had muscles, and droplets of perspiration sprang across her forehead and upper lip. Dabbing these away at least gave me something to do.

Following advice from other new fathers, I tried not to look, but out of the corner of my eye I could see the midwives stretching Sarah's vagina and revealing the crown of the baby's hairy head. The doctor was pleased, but she decided Sarah required an episiotomy to deliver the baby. Too exhausted and anxious about the baby's health to ask any questions, Sarah consented immediately.

## 10.40am

We were finally in the home straight. I was desperate for everything to be ok and for the ordeal to be over for Sarah. Tears welled in my eyes, but I endeavoured to hold them back as I knew they would only worry her.

When the baby was pulled out, they were a terrible combination of purple, blue and grey. They remained silent for a few long seconds and in that time I felt panic growing in the pit of my stomach. The midwives rubbed the baby roughly with a towel, brushing off some of the venix casesoa across their back. The baby then let out a belated loud cry of pure displeasure. As relief washed over me, the mental dam I'd built to hold back the tears began to crumble.

The baby was placed face down to go skin-to-skin with Sarah. As the tension in the room dissipated, one of the midwives asked, "Does anyone know the gender?"

No one had taken the time to look.

When a friend of mine recently became a father, he was given the responsibility of declaring the gender and proudly announced his wife had given birth to a boy. One of the midwives had to gently point out that she hadn't. When I first heard this story, I was incredulous. But when one of the midwives held up the baby for me to do the honours, I realised how easy a mistake it is to make. In the excitement of the moment, the umbilical cord looks a lot like a penis. I looked twice before happily announcing we had a baby girl - just as I'd always imagined.

Following my proclamation, our daughter was put back onto Sarah's chest and I surreptitiously began counting her fingers and toes.

The bones in a baby's skull compress and overlap during birth, giving them a temporarily pointy appearance that's rarely beautiful. As Meg Wolitzer vividly describes in her novel *The Interestings*, the "head gets elongated as it makes the awful soft serve ice cream machine trip through the birth canal".

I'd deliberately tempered my expectations, but I was still taken aback by our baby's appearance. She looked like a crotchety old man with bug eyes projecting out of her extended head. And while the skin on her torso slowly began to resemble a more usual colour, her hands and feet remained dark purple, as if she had been squeezing and stamping on blackberries.

The birth plan we'd completed a few weeks earlier had asked us whether I wanted to cut the umbilical cord and if Sarah wished to have an injection to speed up the delivery of the placenta. We answered yes to both questions - though in regards to the umbilical cord, I did so only after receiving assurances I couldn't cut it incorrectly. Following the injection, it didn't take long for Sarah's placenta to arrive, looking like a huge cut of partially digested steak.

Other questions included whether we wanted our baby to receive a vitamin K injection to prevent a rare but serious disorder called Vitamin K Deficiency Bleeding. Again, the answer was yes, and our baby girl made a clamorous cry as the needle entered her thigh.

She quickly settled when placed back on her mum and Sarah received stitches as they bonded.

When we were alone, I turned to Sarah. "She doesn't look like an Olivia or a Zoe to me. What do you think?"

"No, you're right - she doesn't."

"But I'm leaning towards Zoe. How about you?"

"I like Zoe."

"Shall I message our parents?"

"Please."

Despite feeling exhausted, I couldn't resist the opportunity to set tongues wagging. I announced on my family's Whatsapp group that Sarah had given birth to a baby girl called Regina Armstrong Atkin.

Three minutes later, I revealed the truth. Our baby was to be Zoe Sienna Atkin. Gratifyingly, I learned that afternoon my initial announcement had created the desired effect. My sister had been straight on the phone to Mum, lambasting our choice. Apologies to any Reginas reading this.


*2.15pm*

Sarah's parents arrived and we were moved to the hospital's postnatal ward where Zoe was observed and various measurements taken. Her weight had already been recorded as 8lb 4oz (3.7kg), proving the accuracy of the estimations of the past few weeks. Zoe's height of 54cm put her in the 98th percentile of all newborns, making it all the more remark-able that Sarah had been carrying small.

Due to the length of time between Sarah's waters breaking and Zoe's arrival, the doctors wanted mother and daughter to remain in hospital overnight. We decided it was best I returned home so I could sleep in a bed. Going along with this plan wasn't going to put me in early contention for Dad of the Year, but I'd already fallen asleep while waiting for a midwife to see us. When she arrived, I woke with a start, not having a clue where I was and having forgotten entirely that I'd become a father.


**Day 294, Spring Bank Holiday, Monday 29 May**

After a final few checks on Zoe's hearing and breathing, she and Sarah were discharged and we headed for home. Our tired, wide-eyed grins must have given us away, for on the way out a security guard offered to take a photograph of the three of us.

"Congratulations," he said, handing back my phone. "In case you haven't chosen a name yet, my name's Dave."

# EPILOGUE

When we skipped out of the hospital on that Monday morning, we didn't think we would be back so soon. We lasted just 13 hours.

As was to be expected, Zoe struggled to settle on her first night at home. All babies have something called the Moro reflex, which causes them to appear startled and fling their arms out if they feel they are falling. Newborns often display this when they're going to sleep, but what worried us was that Zoe did this every 20 or 30 seconds and combined it with a tremor that resembled a seizure.

We called the midwife team seeking reassurance. Due to an excess of caution - understandable when dealing with the health of newborns - they advised us to call 999. Which wasn't very reassuring. By midnight we had three paramedics in the house.

They thought Zoe was probably fine, but advised us to go to the hospital's paediatric A&E department to be sure. By 4am the doctors had ruled out the possibility of a seizure, but they detected Zoe had raised lactate levels. When considered in conjunction with the length of time between Sarah's waters breaking and Zoe's birth, the doctors wanted to rule out the possibility of sepsis (a potentially life-threatening reaction to an infection) and asked us to stay overnight for further assessment.

Thankfully, the two factors were found to be unrelated and we were discharged on Tuesday afternoon, hoping to be more successful at staying at home the second time around.

Other than this incident, the first few days went by in a sleep-deprived blur. We lived one day at a time, knowing little of what was going on around us and caring even less. The immediacy and potency of the connection I felt with Zoe amazed me. I can only compare it to when Sarah and I were first dating, when I'd walk around in a daze, not quite believing my luck that this girl had arrived in my life.

Zoe's features changed remarkably quickly and she turned into a beautiful baby within a few days. She is incredibly cute, and never more so than when sleeping curled up like a marsupial, tucking her long legs into her chest, in the position she must have adopted in the womb. Her eyes slowly changed too, from a cold metallic blue, to a dark shade of teal. They are likely to continue to change until Zoe is nine months old, but may not settle completely until she is three.

I still find it hard to comprehend that her beauty is the result of an amalgamation of both Sarah and my genes. As far as we can tell, she doesn't look like either of us.

Scientists remain divided, but many midwives, doctors, researchers and families will vouch that first-born children often look a lot like their father at birth. The theory is that this is an evolutionary characteristic which helps the father to bond with the baby, making it more likely he will take care of them.

Admittedly, it's not a ringing endorsement of a father's inherent parenting skills.

Those who ascribe to the theory suggest the resemblance disappears after a year, by which point the bond between father and baby has been cemented.

Zoe's grandparents fell in love with her immediately. Lola has said she might call her Zsa Zsa, in recognition of Zoe's initials and the nine-time married American actress and socialite Zsa Zsa Gabor. I quite like the nickname and have no doubt that Lola and Zsa Zsa will have a rum time together.

Lola gave us a copy of *The Sunday Times* from the day of Zoe's birth to keep as a memento. Unfortunately it came a cropper when Sarah, knackered from so many overnight feeding sessions and nappy changes, absent-mindedly scribbled across the front page to check whether a pen was working. I've not been immune from lapses in concentration myself. I attended a postnatal appointment with Zoe unaware my shirt was inside out.

When I changed my epilepsy medication, I was warned I might feel more fatigued than normal. I certainly do, but whether this is anything to do with the medication is a moot point.

I remain endlessly entertained by the sheer scale of Zoe's yawn, her expressive contentment after doing a poo and the silkiness of her hair. I didn't think it was possible for anything to feel softer than a dog's ears, but Zoe's already showing me the error of my ways. I want to cherish each moment, but I find it impossible not to look into her eyes and imagine what she might be like when she can walk and talk and what she will be like as a teenager and as a woman. What might she achieve? What will make her happy?

More fundamentally, when I'm holding her I marvel at the simple fact that I've become a daddy. And not just any daddy. Zoe's Daddy.

The adventure has only just begun.

# ACKNOWLEDGMENTS

There would have been little point writing this book without being unflinchingly honest. So I'm extremely grateful to Sarah for permitting me to document these transformative nine months with such freedom. I'm acutely aware many others would not have been so generous.

Collectively, we would like to thank the doctors and midwives who looked after us (and Zoe!) at the Rosie Hospital at Addenbrooke's.

# ALSO BY CHRIS ATKIN

## Escape To California

*He wasn't trying to break America. But would America break him?*

Rocked by political turmoil, climate change and a global pandemic, the US was calling out for a hero. Unfortunately, it was travel writer Chris Atkin who turned up.

Over the course of nearly two years living in the Golden State, Chris explores the history and incredible landscapes of western America.

He learns about the unsolved murder of the co-founder of Stanford University and the pioneer family reduced to cannibalism. He also finds the entrepreneurial spirit at the heart of California, which, for all of Silicon Valley's success stories, is equally central to the tale of how hippies came to benefit when nearly three tonnes of marijuana fell from the skies above Yosemite.

When not living next door to Donkey from Shrek, Chris dodges bears, mountain lions, rattlesnakes and Covid-deniers, and discovers there's more than one way to live the American Dream.

# ALSO BY CHRIS ATKIN

## (Just As Well) It's Not About The Bike

*Discover the untold stories of one of the world's most popular coastlines.*

Part sporting travelogue, part political history, the book follows Chris' 1,300km cycle route from Valencia to Gibraltar. En route, he travels through Spain's most picturesque towns. And Benidorm.

Along the way Chris learns about the region's history, from the time four hydrogen bombs fell over Spain, to the politician who shot General Franco's daughter in the bottom yet rose to become one of the country's most powerful men. While cycling across Spain, Chris also meets an array of eccentric characters such as the man who lives in a cave and the Airbnb host who admitted strangling her previous guest.

People told him he was crazy to leave his job and his girlfriend behind to jump on the cheapest bike he could find. After a series of mishaps including one that almost sparked a mountain rescue mission, it would appear they were right.

# ABOUT THE AUTHOR

Since spending five years working in the television studios at Sky News and BT Sport in London, Chris has worked as a freelance writer.

He has written for numerous publications, including *The Times*, *The Huffington Post* and *Time Out*.

When he's not writing books and articles, Chris works as a copywriter and digital marketer.

In his free time, you'll likely find him discovering somewhere new, or in his garden in Cambridge, tending his vegetable patch while listening out for any noise emanating from the crowd at his beloved Cambridge United.

Printed in Great Britain
by Amazon

43998143R00081